THE GABARDINE GANG

POWER AND BETRAYAL IN HARTFORD'S MOB SCENE

KEVIN DiBACCO

WILDBLUE
PRESS

WildBluePress.com

THE GABARDINE GANG published by:
WILDBLUE PRESS
P.O. Box 102440
Denver, Colorado 80250

ISBN 978-1-960332-68-4 Trade Paperback
ISBN 978-1960332-69-1 eBook
ISBN 978-1-960332-67-7 Hardback

Interior Formatting and Cover Design by Elijah Toten, totencreative.com

THE GABARDINE GANG

TABLE OF CONTENTS

INTRODUCTION   7

1. THE GABARDINE GANG   9
2. THE CENTER OF MY UNIVERSE   13
3. OTHER PLANETS IN MY SOLAR SYSTEM   28
4. THE DANGLING MAN   36
5. HOLIDAY IN THE SUNSHINE STATE   48
6. COMMENCE MISSION: OPERATION
   HOUSE DETOUR: MAINE   62
7. MILK AND BREAD   70
8. HOLIDAY IN THE SILVER STATE   78
9. A TIME OF WONDER   85
10. 1968 - THE PREACHER AND THE MOBSTER   111
11. TAXIS AND BABIES   116
12. HOLIDAY IN THE EMPIRE STATE   126
13 WHEELS AND PELOTAS IN WINDSOR LOCKS   135
14. NO HOLIDAY IN THE NUTMEG STATE   160
15. THE SUPERNOVA EXPLODES   179
16. STARBURST TO BLACK HOLE   194

AFTERWORD   200

INTRODUCTION

Adult conversations often meander into the subject, "What did your father do?" and my response, "He was a mobster," is usually a conversation stopper. While this response frequently derails small talk, it is true. My dad was a small-time organized crime boss for well over twenty years, beginning in the 1950s.

You might have memories of neighborhoods like mine in the North End of Hartford. You remember luncheonettes like Pal's, the place my dad owned and if the topic comes up, you always defend its honor as the best place ever. You watched "The Untouchables" and "Dragnet" on TV and heard tales of mobsters on classic serial radio shows. Those characters' lives were so far removed from yours; they were an exciting escape from reality. But this tabloid header, made for radio, TV and movie life was my life.

The mobsters, illegal activity, racism, sexism, and violence in this book aren't an exercise with artistic license. This is how my life was, and as such, I make no apologies for it. You don't choose the time or family you are born into; you can only play the hand you are dealt.

It's impossible to separate the threads of mobster life with my family life but as a filmmaker and storyteller, I want to document these stories before I get too old to remember them. I had many internal debates before I decided to write this as I knew there was no way to recount my real-life mob stories without also exposing my family dysfunction which was in some part the result of my father's unlikely occupation. But my dad, Geno, is long past, as are all his crew members and I've changed the names of any of my relatives who are still living. My mom, Rena, God rest her soul, passed away in 2011, but I spent many hours with her in her last years. We talked about my memories, which she either confirmed or corrected, and we shared our perspectives about that time, so the stories in this book are as true as the two of us recalled.

Those of you who are interested in the gangster life will appreciate this book because the stories here are all based on real events that occurred in my life until I reached adulthood. Please be advised some of them are graphic.

I hope you are as entertained reading this book as I was writing it. If nothing else, you'll get a sense of what life was like growing up in a different place and time.

1. THE GABARDINE GANG

This is a short story about how the "Gabardine Gang" hailing from Hartford, Connecticut, and headed by Geno, my father, got its name.

The "Gabardine Gang" was a group of guys, mostly Italian, who, in the decades spanning the fifties and sixties, ran an organized crime organization which controlled the dark side of Hartford, Connecticut.

There are about a hundred or so miles between Hartford and New York and another seventy miles between Hartford and New Jersey. Closer to home Providence and Boston crime syndicates made those bigger cities seem far away. Hartford is at the hub of two major interstates that connect all these places, we lived close enough to Boston and New York to know what their bigger organized crime operations were doing and what was making money for them. My dad also kept tabs on the new money-making concepts these larger gangs were involved in.

The Gabardine Gang was a group of small-time gangsters who were nothing like the Mafia guys you've probably heard about. For starters, they were not the glamorous, expensive suit wearing types. In fact, the nickname "Gabardine Gang" stemmed from a joke my mom made the day after a score (stolen goods) delivery I secretly witnessed when I was only about five years old.

A knock on our apartment door woke me up.

I got out of bed in time to peek out of my bedroom door and see a couple of my dad's crew come in carrying about half a dozen brand new Gabardine suits, all assorted colors, still in plastic bags, the tags intact. My parents gathered in the living room as the suits were laid out on the couch. My dad was immediately drawn to a light gray one. Once he tried it on, you could see the two of them became instant friends, although my mom was indifferent to this new infatuation.

Even though he could have easily afforded this suit on his own, my dad kept it, the guys took the rest and left. I was able to close my door before my spying was detected. The next day, my dad brought his new best friend to a local tailor he used on a regular basis and had it custom fit. Dad always wanted things exactly the way he wanted.

A couple of days later, a guy in a new Cadillac pulled up to Pal's, the luncheonette my dad owned and delivered the suit to him. Geno, happy and proud, crossed Barbour Street to our apartment, placed the suit in the closet and went back to Pal's.

My dad was head over heels in love with my mother at that time, and he loved teasing her. I have always believed this was one of the reasons she loved him. Not only could she tolerate his teasing and overall bad behavior, but she could give it as well as she could take it. like, "So the night Dad got his suit back from the tailor, he jokingly told my mom "Some of the girls were stopping by to see the new haul," meaning the two prostitutes who lived underneath us on the second floor, were coming by to see his new suit.

My mom proceeded to bust his chops with a line I'll never forget.

"You bring any of those sluts around here and you will find yourself and your Gabardine Gang out on the street!"

My mother was the only person who could get away with a joke like that and they both laughed at it. "The Gabardine Gang" became a private joke in our family and it stuck in my head. I kept that suit until I was nearly sixty to remind me of those times.

The core members of The Gabardine Gang were my father, Geno; Sonny, my dad's Black bodyguard; Henry, my father's money man and accountant; Johnny "Knucks," a former light heavy weight boxer who often helped Sonny with some of the more physical tasks; John, a Hartford detective on my dad's payroll who helped keep everyone out of trouble; David and Moshe, middle men who moved high-end stolen merchandise; Sam, the butcher who ran the local deli; the Rizzo brothers, two local Italian thugs and about a dozen other characters including Nick "The Fatman," Bob "Meat" (another butcher), David "The Eggplant," Tommy "Pork Chops," Henry "The Carp" and Tony "Ugatz" all of them looked up to my father as a leader.

My dad and his crew of misfits ran their small, but profitable, operation out of Pal's, his luncheonette on Barbour Street in Hartford's North End of Hartford.

The Gabardine operation made money from gambling operations, looting, fencing high-end items, prostitution, and bribery. They also had interests in loan sharking, protection money and a couple other business ventures.

Clearly, they weren't fancy dressers, nor did they live in mansions or have maids and other staff. They were blue collar" mobsters, or as I call them, "low-level gangsters."

Even today, gangsters like this exist in the seedy underbelly of every major city but you will almost never know their names or hear about them on the news. These anonymous people are the backbone of organized crime, and their gangs work your local streets, making a living doing whatever they have to. There are far more of these low-level gangs than there are those with family heads, or godfathers as they're sometimes called in the media and pop culture.

Pal's had a long shiny chrome lunch counter and a greasy spoon menu. The rest of the room was filled with wall-to-wall slot machines and two-way mirrors behind which my dad and his cohorts would assess and plan their business moves in a small, smoke-filled office. Most of the time, I wasn't allowed to be around there when the grown-ups were meeting; I was too young. But I was irrepressible and relentlessly inquisitive about everything and managed to get a first-hand look at what went on in this little luncheonette, some of my dad's other business concerns and in our neighborhood.

2. THE CENTER OF MY UNIVERSE

I have some memories of my early childhood on Barbour Street that are so vivid it's like they happened yesterday. Other recollections come from tales told to me, time after time, first by my father and then by my mother when I was old enough to understand what had happened. When I heard them, I remembered being there and witnessing them. Some other stories are family legends I wasn't present for but heard so often. They are as much a part of my history as anything I have ever said or done. But before I get into them, let me tell you a bit about my neighborhood and the regular cast of characters who were the center of my universe when I was a five-year-old boy. Life in an inner city in the late fifties was decidedly different than inner city culture today. The entire North End of Hartford was about five thousand people living in just a little over three square miles and my neighborhood there was safe and quiet, that's for sure.

It helped that my dad was its crime boss, but overall people were just more respectful of each other back then. Instead of residents stealing from and otherwise taking advantage of people they knew, if only in passing, the neighborhood I was familiar with as a baby boom kid was comprised of civilized, cordial people of character. Except for my dad and the rest of the Gabardine Gang and even then, for the most part, they looked and sounded just like everyone else.

The cars lining the streets were made in America by American companies and were often close to twenty feet long. Women rarely stepped out in slacks, a lady wore a dress or a skirt and fedora hats on men were commonplace. Top of the line televisions only came in black and white. We didn't have cell phones, we had party lines.

Cops were rarely seen on the streets unless they were visiting my dad, but despite this, there was almost no crime. Everyone knew the police were the least of their worries. Dad was the enforcer of a "you protect your own" culture and other than what he and his crew generated, there was pretty much no crime. If you weren't a member of his crew, my dad provided an incentive to behave which differed quite a lot from the police and their threat of jail. Fearing jail was nothing compared to the fear of wondering if some of your body parts would be found and identified should you decide to steal or otherwise take advantage of one of your own and my dad and his guys found out about it.

In an odd but very real way, my dad's policy made everyone feel safe. Women could walk the street alone at all hours, most of the stores and shops stayed open until midnight and you never saw bars on windows or doors.

No one dared steal a vehicle there even though car doors were never locked, and the ignition keys always stayed inside the cars overnight. All the guys in the Gabardine Gang made this a regular habit because they never knew when they'd have to rush out quickly for a job or get home even faster for their wife.

Our home was on Barbour Street in a three story, six-unit apartment building right across the street from Pal's.

I clearly remember our building and all the apartments and tenants in it. It was your basic, non-descript inner city apartment building, exactly like the thousands of others that were constructed as part of the post-World War Two building boom. My dad didn't own the building; he had taken it over as payment for a past-due debt from one of his gambling operations, and he and his gang ran it. The only thing that made our building distinct was the double-plated bulletproof glass in the three tall, narrow windows on the first floor.

When you're a kid, everything seems huge. But I'm not mistaken about the glass in our living room windows being much thicker than anyone else's. I was told that only the first floor had bulletproof windows because it was so close to the street. However, even the windows in our apartment seemed thicker than normal.

The back of the building had a huge outside wooden stairway and each apartment had a porch. There were chairs on all the porches and even a card table or two so the guys could have their meetings outside when it was hot. We didn't have air conditioners, but my dad had purchased huge industrial fans for each floor, one in the front and one in the back and between all of them they kept the place cool in the summer. The fans would pull air in from the front of the building and suck it out the other side. Back then, everyone smoked and there was always cigar and cigarette smoke thickening the air at the backside of the building where the exhaust units were. The fans were very noisy and a little intimidating because to me they looked like giant airboat motors. Despite this, I slept like a baby to their constant hum and to this day, I need background noise like an air conditioner or fan to get to sleep.

We lived on the third floor in a two-bedroom apartment and there was a common hallway linking all the apartments together. Fire laws were in their infancy back then and the landings were always cluttered with an overflow of my toys: fire trucks, bikes with training wheels and other childhood booty I accumulated as a spoiled only child.

Our apartment was as nondescript as the building it was in. Blue collar mobsters were working class people just like everyone else. It was only how they made their living that was different.

The living room had a comfortable overstuffed sofa and a matching loveseat, both of which were regularly replaced due to the steady flow of smoking and eating guests who left stains and burn holes that would defeat the most durable of fabrics. We had a seemingly endless supply of lace furniture scarves and doilies Italian ladies in the neighborhood gave Mom and she would spruce things up and hide the more than occasional flaw. My mother loved to sew and so we often had new curtains she made when she found some fabric she liked, or she wanted to change this up for the change of seasons. We had a giant black and white television. You'd have to wait to warm up before the picture came on, beginning with a little white dot in the middle which would slowly spread across the screen like a grayscale sunset. Next to it was a hi-fi turntable stereo system well hidden in a big wooden cabinet that also held all my parents' record albums. Dean Martin (his records played all the time after my parents met him in Las Vegas and bought all his records), Frank Sinatra and Perry Como for my dad and my mom's collection of Hank Williams, Marty Robbins, and Johnny Cash. Ashtrays were scattered everywhere and there were cigarette lighters ensconced in ceramic holders the size of a coffee mug. They were huge but you never worried about misplacing them!

A bottomless percolator coffee pot was always on in the kitchen, and if the stove ever had a free burner, I don't remember it. Rena, my mom, loved to cook, and she was great at it. There was always tomato sauce or soup on the stove and something in the oven. The countertops and the kitchen table were cluttered with knick-knacks my mom would buy on one of our many road trips. We had a couple of dozen sets of salt and pepper shakers.

Obviously, one bedroom belonged to my parents, and I rarely had occasion to go in there. The other bedroom was decorated with cowboy items. I was a huge Roy Rogers fan. Once Mom even brought me back some real cowboy garb from one of my parent's occasional trips to Las Vegas.

To say Geno, my dad, was unlike other dad's would be an understatement. He was a short, stocky, prematurely bald man who loved being the ruler of his little kingdom in Hartford's North End and if you could help him out, he was the nicest guy ever. Big tips, lots of perks and parties for his friends and gang. My mom told me that for a long time he would shower her with gifts, furs, and trips across the country.

My dad had three brothers who all had "real jobs." Tony was a master electrician and he wired much of the new construction in the city of Hartford. Julio was a master glass cutter who also was involved in the new construction while Arturo was a printer. We would see them on holidays and on our rounds of weekly visits. The only time I ever saw my father cry was when Arturo called one day to tell him Tony had died.

But as his dealings with organized crime became more widespread, my dad went from being hip for the time to being someone you wouldn't want your worst enemy to meet.

Like Al Capone and "Lucky" Luciano who were also short gangsters, height wasn't a good barometric measure of his personality. Geno, (or "Whitey" as my father was nicknamed because he disliked anyone of color) packed a world of mean into his five-foot eight frame.

As I look back on all the people that I have come across in my life, I can honestly say, my dad was unlike anyone I have ever met. While I have a few fond childhood memories about him, overall, he was cold, calculating, and uncaring to the point of being almost robotic. He never said, "I love you" to anyone, not even my mom. A lot of our friends and neighbors feared him because he was very unpredictable. One minute he'd be joking with you and the next, he'd have you up against the wall by the neck if he took the slightest offense. Many people thought he was pure evil and stayed as far away from him as possible. A few others thought his little kingdom and his authority in it was just a sham and challenged him. This never worked out well for them.

My dad was just a mean human being. He only cared about himself and what was in it for him. If you weren't on his program, he hated you and would have you beat up just for looking at him wrong.

My mother, Rena, was gorgeous. She had flowing auburn hair, big blue eyes and an hourglass figure poured into a size five dress. When she walked into a room, everyone noticed and many people who met her said she was prettier than Rita Hayworth, a famous movie star of those times. But she was so much more than that.

Rena was the nicest person in the world and almost always seemed to be helping someone without a second thought or expecting a favor down the line. In many ways, she and my dad were opposites. She would give a free lunch to strangers at Pal's and would frequently donate some of my dad's overstock to charity. My mom was a woman of many skills.

As a Maine native, my mother loved seafood. Lobster, shrimp, scallops, she couldn't get enough of it, so it was always a staple in our household. There was also not an Italian dish you can name she couldn't cook to perfection. My dad gave her recipes which had been in his family for generations, and she mastered every single one of them: red sauce, lasagna, homemade sausage and peppers to name just a few. Since there was a steady stream of people constantly in and out of our apartment, especially at night, Mom had four or five courses available almost every night and this kept her in the kitchen a lot.

But baking was where she really excelled. Bread, pies, cake, there was always something in the oven. At one point, she even entertained the idea of opening her own bakery, but my dad was too cheap to help her with the startup money.

Geno and Rena met when she was waitressing at a nightclub where he was a regular. At the time, she had just gotten out of an abusive marriage and her service in the Air Force as a Meteorologist. (She was always able to predict the weather just by looking at the clouds. I remember she predicted the huge tornado which raced through our small town of Windsor Locks back in 1979.) After her divorce, she moved to Hartford to stay with her sister Barbara and with her good looks, cooking skills and kind heart, she certainly stuck out in that city. No doubt she could have dated anyone she wanted.

Politicians, millionaires, and mobsters up and down the East Coast asked her to fly with them around the country. In fact, Anthony Barile, the Rhode Island crime boss tied to the infamous New York Genovese Mafia family (one of the legendary Five Families), which was headed by Lucky Luciano when I was a boy, fell in love with her and was actively chasing her at the same time as my dad. You would think her choice would have been a no-brainer—one was a millionaire, and the other was just a blue-collar gangster. But my mom followed her heart and used her feminine wiles to pit them against each other for her hand in marriage by using Barile's interest in her to pressure my dad to commit to her. She and my dad lived together for a brief time until she was positive, he was the man for her although later my mom would kid, she married the wrong gangster. They married in 1959, a year after they met.

As for the other tenants in the building...

Charlie lived in the apartment across the hall from us. He was a drifter and a drunk who did building maintenance for my dad. He was always in trouble and finally his daughter decided to take him in with her and he moved to New Haven, Connecticut with her. After he moved out, Shirley moved into the apartment and became a big part of our lives. My mom wasn't able to socialize much as my dad kept her under his thumb. When Shirley arrived, my mom finally had someone she could confide in and talk to. Someone that was normal and not part of the organized crime world. You might know that my mom was enjoying having a faithful friend to talk to.

Directly downstairs from us was Dotty, a cute nursing student with long brown hair and blue eyes. She was also what people today would describe as my fulltime nanny.

I know it seems odd I basically had a full-time nanny, given I was an only child, and my mom didn't have a job outside of the house. But there was more than enough work to keep my mom busy all the time as she made sure the "hospitality" end of my father's businesses ran smoothly. There were six apartments in our building, plus Pal's and the Little Casino across the street. Her job was to keep all of them stocked with food and whatever else they needed, including booze and restaurant/bar supplies. In those days there were no reps to stop in and restock Pal's. She was on the road every day (except when there was snow—then Dad would send one of his guys out) with a roll of cash, going to the city's bakers, butchers, and dozens of other suppliers to get everything we needed. She also helped Dad with the books for both Pal's and the Little Casino. I was too young to go to school so that's how Dotty fit right in.

Dotty came to us highly recommended by a friend of my mother's but that didn't stop Mom from putting her through the wringer and thoroughly checking her out before she agreed to hire her. When she wasn't taking care of me, Dotty spent a lot of time with her boyfriend Bob who my parents liked a lot. He was always visiting us, even when Dotty wasn't around, and my dad made sure he was always protected.

My mom treated Dotty like a daughter and was always taking her shopping. When she redecorated Charlie's old place, Mom made her matching curtains in her favorite colors. She was with me more than my mother, that's for sure, and she tucked me into bed every night.

Across the hall from her lived two good-looking prostitutes who worked for my dad. I didn't see them much. They usually went to bed extremely late and didn't get up before lunch time.

Downstairs on the first floor were two empty apartments where no one lived but which were almost always in use. One apartment had a frilly, warm feel and a bedroom with bright floral curtains, valances, and a matching bedspread. It even had pink bathroom fixtures!

The other apartment was less inviting. There was really no difference between the living room and the bedroom. Between these two rooms were three or four televisions, a bunch of telephones, card tables, simple couches as well as a ton of soft chairs and folding chairs. The kitchen had two refrigerators my mom always kept stocked full of food and beer. Even at my youthful age, I knew this was not normal. These two ground floor apartments were off limits for me, although of course, since they were off limits, I snuck into them whenever I could. But technically, I only got to see them when my mom would go into them to restock the refrigerators and clean up.

With all the space in our building, it had been easy enough for Dad and his guys to convert the downstairs into two "vice rooms." My dad's clients didn't need anything fancy—a "man cave" where they could bet on the horses and the games and a separate apartment with nice women who were available to take care of their other needs. When I was older, I learned the nice apartment on the first floor was set up as a place for the girls who lived on the second floor and worked for my dad to party with their tricks who just happened to be guests of my dad with plenty of cash on hand. These high roller friends of my father's would come from out of town to gamble and then relax with girls afterwards. The two prostitutes that lived downstairs from us used that apartment for their boudoir business which was run by my father. The other one, with its phones and TVs, was an old school betting parlor.

I think you have an idea of about half of the operation when I first started figuring things out. There was a constant stream of people entering and leaving our building and our apartment. Everyone who was ever there either worked for my dad or did business with him.

The Game Room was like a one stop shop for illegal activity, and it was no more than fifty yards away from Pal's, Dad's luncheonette, and the Little Casino, the other two places that were the other half of his neighborhood operation. The "Little Casino" as I call it was a mini version of a Vegas betting room. Slot machines lined the walls along with brand new roulette tables, crap tables, blackjack tables and even a fully stocked bar. A small buffet of food was always put out. There was no reason for anyone to go anywhere else. Vending machines sold cigarettes and cigars were always available.

Pal's was my dad's entree into organized crime and when I look back on it, it was an amazingly easy and logical transition for him to make. He was born and brought up in the North End of Hartford, not far from our apartment on Barbour Street. His parents already had family living there. Grandma and Grandpa moved there and settled in directly from Pratola Peligna, Italy, a small town in the central part of the country, which was heavily bombed during World War Two, causing many of its residents to relocate.

Geno was good at gambling, particularly dice games or "craps" and from an early age, gambling had a hold on him. He quit school in the eighth grade to organize his own crap games and he also idolized Lucky Luciano head of the Genovese crime family, one of America's famous Mafia's Five Families. No one who knew him from those days was surprised when he started a gang of his own.

In the mythology of his childhood my father constructed, he got involved with these crap games. Craps is basically a dice game where people wager on the outcome of a pair of rolled dice. This is how my dad started this shady business. He became a Craps king to bring money home to his family, but it's pretty clear, as evidenced by my grandmother throwing him out of the house and leaving him to fend for himself when he was fifteen, skirting the law and making easy money for himself was something he was inextricably drawn to from a very young age. I don't remember much about my grandmother other than that she hated my mother, and whenever she saw her, she would curse at her in Italian. Grandma DiBacco was so mean she made The Wicked Witch in *The Wizard of Oz* look like a saint.

When he was old enough to get a real job, my dad got a union position working for Hartford's public works department. Back then, unions and mobsters worked pretty much hand in hand and through this job, he met many of the city's politicians and union bosses. My dad quickly learned which politicians and other local leaders could be influenced and this information became invaluable as his union connections and entrepreneurial gangster heart led to his introduction to William Grasso, (relative of Ella Grasso, a governor of Connecticut) also from Hartford who had some ties to a large mobster gang, the Barile's from Rhode Island. This gang was headed by Geno's meeting them was a match made in Heaven!

His new friends in Rhode Island told him Hartford only had petty thieves and thugs and was therefore untapped for organized crime. They were instrumental in helping my dad establish himself as the mob boss of Hartford. The Bariles lent him money to buy Pal's, which was already a working restaurant and from there, with their assistance, my dad set it up as a front for gambling. As for the local riffraff who preceded his operation, they were either chased out of the neighborhood or went to work for him.

As a result of this connection, over the years, my dad became known as an "Associate" for the Barile gang. He would move stolen goods every now and then for them and he also raced his horses in Rhode Island on occasion. In return, they would come over to Connecticut a couple times a year and visit my dad's exceptionally talented prostitutes and blow money out the wazoo in the Little Casino when they came here. The Bariles wanted to have Dad more involved at their end, but he didn't want to expand and expose himself to the larger branch of their clan in Boston. He tried to keep his Hartford organization small and controllable. But the deciding factor for him ultimately was he hated taking orders from anyone. That was a big reason he didn't jump into bed with the Rhode Island and Boston groups. He had to be in control and if he joined them outright, he knew he would just be another bottom feeder in another organization. For that reason, he liked being an asshole and would take on freelance jobs as they came along.

Geno opened Pal's around 1957 and he owned it for about ten years until we moved to Windsor Locks. When I say this was the most popular place in the North End, I'm not exaggerating. It was the hot spot for years in the city.

Pal's got its name because back then, cool people would commonly refer to their friends as "Pal's." "Pal" was one of the few pleasant words I heard a lot from my dad. There was no shortage of slang and swears I picked up on when I was around my dad and his guys. Mom tried to limit my exposure to this bad language but that only worked so much.

These guys had slurs for every ethnic group. The Blacks were called "Moulinyans," "Buffalos" or "eggplant." Jews were call "Himeys" or "Beanies." They called their own Italian people "whops," "dagos," "grease balls" and "guineas." Homosexuals were "Fanukes." The list goes on and on, but these were the words I heard every day, generously mixed in with English although when conversations got serious, they would speak only in Italian, but I heard those words then too.

There was a row of four or five large plate glass windows fronting Pal's long, narrow interior. Almost everything in there was chrome, from the long countertop lined with enough chrome chairs and stools to seat almost two dozen people to all the appliances behind it which were chrome as well. This spotless place always glowed under rows of overhead fluorescent tube lighting. The rest of the room was filled with wall-to-wall slot machines and a couple of two-way mirrors which were in front of a little room hidden in the luncheonette's backroom where my dad and his gang kept an eye on things and reviewed and planned their business.

Pal's was always packed for breakfast and lunch, and it was known for the Italian subs my dad would make. Our neighborhood was mostly blue-collar workers and their families, and they all loved my mom and her food! She always had music blasting (Hank Williams was her favorite but if my father was around, there was always a good dose of Frank Sinatra) and it was great fun until closing time at two or three in the afternoon. A few hours later, my dad would go back over and open the "Little Casino" in the basement. That building had traffic going pretty much all day and night!

The "Little Casino" is the term I use to refer to Pal's basement, but my dad just called it "the backroom" which was a term he and his friends used for any room that was used for gambling or whatever else they had going on. As a curious kid I was able to sneak down to the "Little Casino" a few times. Before my mom and dad finally set up a guard to ban me permanently.

That day, I had been a persistent, stubborn, pain in the ass and insisted Dotty take me over there. She did, and Dotty got blasted by my dad. They had just talked about keeping me away from the "Little Casino" a few days earlier and I begged Dotty to let me in. I was never allowed down there again. Dotty never even let me get close!

But I saw enough to remember that under cool bar lights, there were two walls lined with dozens of slot machines. I thought they were just large versions of the cash register which sat on the counter of the luncheonette. Another wall was lined with colorful card tables and in front of the last wall was a nice black leather bar with matching leather stools. One corner had a big roulette wheel, all shiny and new. There was a sexy waitress serving drinks; cigar and cigarette smoke filled the air which was pulled out of the room by large built-in exhaust fans, just like the ones in our apartment building. It wasn't until years later when I was a bit older, wiser, and much more curious I realized exactly what all the set-up downstairs was.

While everyone loved the food at the luncheonette and gaming at the Little Casino, those weren't the biggest money makers in the Pal's building. Loan sharking was the most profitable. Mom and Dad came up with their own system to keep track of the books at that end. All the loan denominations were named after popular movie stars and singers. Gina Lollobrigida was $5000, Frank Sinatra, $1000, and Johnny Cash, Hank Williams, Dean Martin, they, too, had a dollar value attached to their names in this bookkeeping system. As part of this system, the date payments were also recorded backwards. For example, a notation "BG- GinaL 153 and 223" meant Bobby Guilano borrowed $5000 and payments were due on March 15 and March 22.

Sonny, my dad's bodyguard, was at the Little Casino all the time, when he wasn't doing something for my dad. Of all the guys in the gang, Sonny was my favorite and when he was around, I felt like I was surrounded by Fort Knox. He was a massive Black guy an ex-football player who was rumored to have once been drafted for the New York Giants, but he was more well known for being, as *The Bridgeport Telegram* once described him, "one of Hartford's greatest talents at wriggling out of jams."

He looked like a mountain to me, but all six seven and three hundred pounds of him loved me to death and whenever I saw him, he would throw me over his shoulder and walk around the neighborhood. Carrying me around was nothing for him. Our slot machines weighed over two hundred pounds each and Sonny could carry one of them by himself. If anyone needed anything moved, Sonny was the first guy they called.

Everybody loved Sonny. They had no choice.

Not only was Sonny big, but he was also about as mean as a man can come, which is probably one of the reasons why he and my dad got along so well. Sonny never thought twice about punching out anyone he deemed a threat to my dad or our family.

Sonny was paid to protect all of us, most importantly, my dad. He was closer to my father than almost anyone I had ever met. That spoke volumes to me. After all the bragging about how Italians are the superior people, my dad was surround by every other nationality and ethnic makeup.

"Sonny thinks of your dad as his brother," my mom would tell me. "He would take a bullet for him anytime." Which in fact happened at least once that I witnessed with my own eyes.

Strangely enough, my dad felt the same way about Sonny, even though Geno was a pro Italian kind of guy. If you were Italian, you could do no wrong in his book. That's not to say my dad didn't work with everyone because he did, but for as long as I can remember, Sonny was the only Black guy ever allowed in our apartment.

Even when your dad is a mobster, as a young child your exposure to life is limited and mine was no exception. I had my parents, Dotty, and Sonny, and that was all I really needed or knew. I'm sure this was mostly my mother's doing, although my dad certainly went along with it. Eventually, I started to notice other people who regularly came in and out of their lives and to me, they were like planets rotating around our Barbour Street universe.

3. OTHER PLANETS IN MY SOLAR SYSTEM

Like any other organization, the Gabardine Gang had several members whose work was critical to keep things running smoothly. One of the most important of these people was my dad's right-hand man, Henry.

Money was what bonded all these people together. My dad made it and used it. The person who kept track of all these complicated and illegal transactions was Henry.

Henry was a Jewish businessman who grew up with my dad. The Jews and Italians were kindred souls. They all lived together in harmony. My dad was always loyal to those he grew up with in his old North End neighborhood. Henry was constantly looking at books and charts and controlled the numerous metal money boxes which were constantly being moved around from the apartment building to the luncheonette to cars. I never knew exactly what he did, other than collecting and counting cash, Henry was in charge.

He had a beautiful wife and an even more beautiful girlfriend. The guy's always teased Henry if it weren't for his money, with his looks, he'd be lucky to get a date. His girlfriend was some sort of model from New York, and he paraded her around all the time while his wife was at home watching their kids. That's just how these guys were. Like my dad, Henry always drove a brand-new Cadillac and you could tell by the way he lived he was obviously making money with my dad.

Johnny K, also known as "Johnny Knucks," was my dad's best friend and another person he grew up with. Johnny K was an old school light heavyweight boxer, but he would sometimes fight heavy weights as well. He had been hit in the head so many times he couldn't speak well, had a cauliflower ear and a broken nose which spread across his face. In short, he looked like "a hot-headed Italian boxer who was otherwise an average guy" right out of Hollywood casting. His boxing career had made him somewhat of a celebrity in the city and he would tell me stories about his fights (two in Madison Square Garden), how many times he got cut and how in those days, fifteen round matches were very normal. I liked him a lot and he always brought me a gift when he visited.

Even though he hadn't been a professional boxer in years, Johnny K still loved the sport. Not only did he share his stories with me, but he loved teaching his sons to box, and he was always my good-natured sparring partner as I grew up. For over sixty years, he trained hundreds of amateur boxers at two gyms in Hartford. He also loved having lunch with my dad and his friend Willie Pep, a retired featherweight champion of the world. They would sit around talking about past fights and the latest odds-on upcoming ones. Every now and then the three of them would grab a couple of the guys and head out to fights at Madison Square Garden.

Johnny K was in love with my mom, or so I believed back then because while he always gave me a little gift when he came to visit, he always had a small present for her as well. I wondered if my dad ever noticed the boxes of candies, he brought her and that he hung around the luncheonette more than most other people.

By now, you're probably wondering how my father was able to get away with all his shady dealings with no problem. As I said, through his union work, he had been able to find out which politicians were corrupt and once he knew that bribes for them, (including his start-up buddy William Grasso), to grant favors or simply looking the other way were just a regular business expense as far as he was concerned. I was never told if my dad had judges on the payroll but looking back, I'm sure that he had allies in higher places than I knew.

Other than Sonny and Johnny K, there was one other member of Dad's core group who was the linchpin of the organization and the real reason why my dad and his guys never got into trouble. Detective John, my dad's oldest and one of his dearest friends.

John was a Hartford detective and he and his partner Sal were both well-paid members on my dad's payroll. It was because of them the luncheonette and apartment building were never raided or a member of the Gabardine Gang was ever arrested.

John and Sal basically just turned their heads when it came to anything suspicious going on in the neighborhood. They had a tacit and perfectly understandable understanding with my dad it would look bad if people witnessed them acting otherwise. The only time John, Sal and my dad were ever together publicly at our holiday parties was when all our friends, family and neighbors mixed and mingled. It was simply understood if everyone involved helped my dad and respected his rules, there would never be a problem. Cops and gangsters got along; it was a different time.

Privately however, John and Sal would eat dinner with us at least a couple of times a week while they were on duty then disappear with my dad across the street to the Little Casino afterward. They were protectors of the fort, but John was much more to us than a business associate. When John needed something, Dad was right there for him, and John did the same for my dad both personally and for his operations. Our families saw each other regularly, especially on birthdays and holidays.

I remember one time when John and Sal brought at least a dozen cops to the Little Casino and later, The Game Room, for a bachelor party. Police cars were lined up all down the street. What my mom told me many years later was my dad had given them an open bar. When I learned that, it explained why when I woke up the next morning after that party, I found a few of the cops sleeping in the empty apartments. They had been too tanked to leave.

My dad was a Teflon Don, but the good relationship he had with the local police went beyond having two detectives on his payroll. All the cops loved the free lunch he always gave them at Pal's (some days it seemed like the entire force was there), but more importantly, they all loved my mom. She was quite the looker in those days, but looking at her was as far as anyone got. Everyone knew flirting with her wouldn't be good for them health wise.

As my dad's operation expanded, he brought in a couple of other core members of his crew like David.

David was a savvy Jewish businessman and one of my father's "behind the scenes" guys. My dad believed since David was Jewish, he was good with making money which is why he always let him control much of his operations finances at the selling end of things. When Dad began expanding his business, his crew began robbing big trucks. Big trucks were targeted because hijacking trucks full of new products was profitable. His guys were particularly good at it. And they never got caught for these acts because of Detective John and his police connections.

When the crew hijacked a truck; jewelry, alcohol, cigarettes, furs, and electronics being the usual targeted items, David would evaluate the product and move it. Anything other than clothing (that's a part of the operation you'll learn about in a minute), was his deal. He knew exactly what a haul was worth and through his network, sold it at fair market value. He went to all the crew's homes as well and they would buy these stolen goods at pennies on the dollar. Excluding tax, of course.

We only saw David on Sunday when we would make our weekly trip to his house. When we visited him and his family, he and my dad would go to his basement office and leave my mom and I with his wife and kids. I never liked going there, but it was on the rounds of places we would stop in on the weekends.

Another one of my dad's inside guys was Moshe, another childhood friend. Moshe would move the clothing items only. When we lived in Hartford, he would visit my dad at Pal's and pick up all the clothing ready to be moved and integrate the hot items into the regular stock in his clothing store.

To me, this was the coolest job of all, especially after we moved to the country. When we were on Barbour Street, he would stop in and see my dad at Pal's and coordinate the merchandise that was constantly moving during the week but once we moved to Windsor Locks, he changed his business model which became a wonderful retail outlet for him, my dad, and his crew.

Moshe would spend three days a week on the road going to high-end customers' homes and selling his clothing line. His clientele were people with money who always paid in cash and had no time to go shopping. If you needed a fur coat, he had it. If you needed a dress shirt, he had it. Hats. He had them too. He made it a point to go to his customers with racks of clothing and accessories and set up his display in their living room, integrating the hot furs and suits boosted by my dad's crew. Moshe would incorporate much of my father's stolen items into his own line of merchandise. Moshe was like a traveling Bloomingdales, bringing high end clothing right in the privacy of client's homes. This was a huge help in the operation's ability to move stolen products. The buyers never questioned if the furs or anything else were stolen as long as there was the manufacturer's tags and name brands on them.

Moshe was the best salesman I've ever met. He would move all their stolen items in a week or two. Then there was Sam "The Butcher." I saw him a lot because his market was right next to Pal's.

He was always wearing a bloody apron.

Always.

When Sam shook your hand, you thought it had been crushed in a machine press or rolled over by a truck. He had the biggest, fattest hands I had ever seen and had a grip like a gorilla.

All I knew was Sam supplied all the meats for the luncheonette and the apartment. Now that I think about it, he supplied the meat for most of the North End. We always had fresh Italian sausage, roast beef, pork, gabagool, sirloin, you name it, on hand.

I'm pretty sure Sam was not just a butcher, though. While I'd like to believe he was simply that, there were many times when Sam was at places not related to his shop, wearing his bloody apron. The apron was part of the uniform he wore when he went around collecting money for my dad. Between his sheer size and choice of accessories, Sam was an effective collector. Sam wasn't squeamish about blood, and this was important to my dad's guys, that's for sure.

There were some other notable members of the crew I would only see on occasion, like the Rossi brothers who were my dad's strong arms, always on the road, always looking for a fight. I only saw them on the holidays and special occasions. One was an ex-boxer, and they were two of the meanest bastards I have ever met. Even when I saw them at the house for Christmas, I was unsure about them, so I kept my distance. They were typical loud and obnoxious Italians. Neither of them had a conscience nor a concept of law and either one of them would have killed their own grandmother if the price was right. These were not guys you wanted to piss off.

It was much later in life. I went to college with one of their nephews. Once I found out he was related to "the" Hartford Rossi's, we got to talking. I had long lost touch with them, but from him I learned his uncles spent all their lives living the same way they did in the fifties and sixties: mean until the very end.

My mom, Rena, had her own friends as well. She needed all the help she could get to endure the circus which went along with being married to my father. Having people around she could trust not to talk about what they knew about my dad's business was the only way she could cope and her best friend, Shirley, was invaluable in that regard.

Shirley was a world class Italian/Cuban beauty all the guys went crazy over. She had been a contestant in the 1953 Miss Florida pageant, but she was more than just a beauty queen. She was a genuinely nice person; beautiful, smart, and kind. I think my dad had a crush on her.

My parents met her on one of their many trips to Florida on the horse track circuit. She was working for one of my dad's friends when unfortunately, she landed in an abusive marriage. When my parents caught wind of it, they immediately made plans to get her out of Florida and brought her back to Connecticut with them on their last trip there. She was protected like a member of our family and had access to all my parents' things: cars, furs, money, and the apartment building. She adjusted to life in Connecticut nicely and lived with us for a couple of months until Charlie from the apartment across from us moved out and she moved into there.

Shirley and my mom were inseparable, and my mom made sure Shirley was always taken care of. She waitressed at Pal's and would also hostess at the Little Casino. She made terrific tips from both places and always had a good-sized wad of cash on her. She eventually bought her own white Cadillac and would drive my mom around in it. Guys drooled when they saw the two of them driving around in that.

Having Dotty and Shirley around was like having one big extended family! Everybody got along, especially with Dotty who was like the sister they never had. Those two girls had it made as long as they just did their jobs, and their jobs were great. Mom and Dad paid all their bills, they could never get a traffic ticket, no one in law enforcement could mess with them. They got cars, furs, furniture, booze, trips, whatever they wanted! This was a nice ride for both of them and neither ever made any waves.

These were the people and places that I spent my childhood years in and around. It was the kingdom my dad built, and I was its little prince: coddled, spoiled, always as snug as a bug in a rug and always asking questions about everything.

4. THE DANGLING MAN

I started to understand the true nature of our neighborhood, my dad, and the rest of the Gabardine Gang's role in it when I was just a young boy, five or six years old. It was just a couple of years before we moved to the suburbs that I finally did grasp what I was seeing and what I was being shielded from seeing.

Granted, that's the age where most of us have their first "real" memories but mine are unique. Most people can tell you about eating paste in kindergarten, stuff like that, but this was about the time I had been exposed to things enough to realize my neighborhood wasn't like other nice Italian neighborhoods and my dad certainly wasn't like any other dads.

All of America, including Hartford's North End was going through a transitional time in the early 1960s. Either the Italians who lived on my street or the Jews on the next block over owned almost all the buildings and businesses on Barbour Street. If you weren't either of those two ethnic groups it was ok to own any business or property in that neighborhood, if nothing else, you were white. This environment had nothing to do with legal or mandated segregation. Simply put, none of the white locals wanted other races in the neighborhood, especially the growing Black population. That's just how it was in those days. Every group had their own area, and they liked it that way. An unspoken code grew around this principle and stayed that way for years. In fact, some Italian sections of Hartford do their best to preserve that code to this day.

I was told this all changed in my immediate neighborhood when one Jewish family broke tradition and sold a building to a Black business owner.

This single transaction is said to mark the beginning of a permanent change in the North End. Many old timers, both Italian and Jewish, were shocked about this transaction and felt they had been betrayed by one of their own. The Jewish guy who sold his building to a Black man became the most hated man in the city, especially in our neighborhood, and his life was threatened many, many times.

The brick building in question was a two-story high rise about six blocks away from us. Its new owner was named Willie and word got out he planned to renovate it and turn it into a small jazz club. In those days, Hartford was known for having a lively jazz scene. Many of the hottest acts in the music business would stop there while they were coming or going to New York City or Boston because it was an easy break from travel and a good way to make some extra money in between larger gigs.

Every now and then, Dad and I would drive by and watch men work on the building. While I was fascinated by the noise and machinery, Geno wanted to keep close tabs on what they were doing.

Rumor had it this was going to be a "classy joint" for an upscale clientele and from the work I saw being done and all the nice furniture and other trappings I saw being brought in, I believed it.

Truth be told, calling it a "classy joint" was a kinder description than it deserved. But you have to keep in mind the Barbour Street neighborhood. Most of the neighbors were salt of the earth, blue collar people so their idea of a classy joint is akin to saying Denny's is classier than McDonald's.

But it was a cut above many of the small mom and pop watering holes in the neighborhood, although I have some doubts about its legality. Like all bars at the time, women weren't allowed to sit at the bar, so having booths, tables and live entertainment upstairs meant women patrons were welcome there.

While many of the long-term Italian and Jewish residents there, particularly older ones, despised losing ground on a territory that had been theirs for over a hundred years, I remember my dad and his crew were excited about having a secondary hangout.

Once Dad was assured this wasn't going to be a slip shod operation, he and Willie hit it off, despite Willie being Black. I always had a problem understanding this, but my mom always said my dad was color blind to people he really liked (and he pretty much only liked you if it was business related) and hated everyone else.

Looking back, Dad and Willie had quite a few things in common. First, Willie was a hard worker and Dad liked that about anyone. But as they began to get better acquainted, they became friends and business associates.

You see, Willie was cut from the same piece of Gabardine as my dad. While he was true to his word about the club and it became an extremely popular place with forward-thinking locals, Willie was playing another angle which was more of a sure money maker than owning a small, underground jazz club.

He had women.

Beautiful Black and Hispanic women he brought with him from the South. Florida, I believe. He saw a business opportunity for him and them in Hartford.

Some people might have felt this new prostitution business could be an intrusion on their turf or business, but not my dad. Willie needed a friend who could offer the kind of protection against angry locals my dad and his crew were more than able to provide, while my dad saw Willie and his enterprise as another cash cow for them for several reasons.

Dad already has his own prostitutes who worked next to the Game Room but once he had access to the influx of Willie's women, he had a pool of a more diverse group of girls. And most of those new girls needed furs, clothing, jewelry, just the kinds of things Dad happened to have broad access to and were also money makers for him. I remember Willie's girls always looked nice, thanks to my dad, even though their skirts and tops were always tighter, and they showed more skin than any of the other neighborhood women.

The club became quite a hit. Dad, his crew and their Goomahhs (mistresses or girlfriends) became regulars at Willie's, with their own booth and everything always on the house. They would listen to cool jazz and drink the night away while Willie's girls, who Mom said always looked sexy, would buy things from them to attract customers.

There were other people in the neighborhood who were also excited about the new club and in no time, twenty or thirty white Italian, Irish and Jewish locals were mixing with the Black patrons, and everyone got along great.

Business was booming for my dad and Willie as well. Willie would traffic people over to the Little Casino (many of the Black men became regulars there and at Pal's) and Dad would send them back over to the club to drink.

At one point they even talked about combining their businesses into one building, but they decided the system they had designed worked so well they should leave it alone.

This isn't to say things were perfect.

People resistant to change vandalized and tried to rob the jazz club many times in the first few months it was open but by then, my dad and Willie were good friends. Besides, above anything else, my dad knew what was good for Willie's business was good for him so several times he even helped Willie out financially when the club was compromised.

Once Dad made you his friend, he would go all out for you and Willie was like that too.

Geno also instituted his own unique system for controlling potential problems. He began by always having a couple groups of his guys both inside and outside Willie's club to keep an eye out for trouble. Both the Little Casino and Willie's operated well into the night, so it was easy enough for my dad to send a couple of whatever neighborhood guys that were hanging out at the Little Casino to patrol the streets. These were considered entry level jobs into my dad's crime organization and these guys were always thrilled to do it to get a foot in the door. He also took things a step further with some of the more belligerent people and made Pal's and the Little Casino off limits to those who were causing trouble and trying to drive Willie out.

Overall, my dad's protection helped Willie immensely, although it was not without its drawbacks. I heard my parents caution Willie more than once about being perceived as an "Uncle Tom" by some of the other Black neighbors. Willie didn't seem to care about that and to return Dad's protection favor, he would have his guys protect Pal's and the Little Casino when they were both closed.

But most people in the neighborhood weren't profiting from these changes like my dad was and so they didn't see things the way he did. More and more building owners sold their property to get out of the area, which of course led to more Black families moving in. The more Black families that moved in, the more obvious and vocal the resentment from old timers became and this obviously didn't go over well with the new residents who were accustomed to a warmer climate, both physically and emotionally.

Straddling the middle of the road wasn't easy for Geno on this one.

He needed to keep the peace because fights and vandalism in the neighborhood weren't good for business. But then he figured out how to preserve and enhance his reputation in the community, keep the peace and make even more money.

His solution was quite simple.

Many local business owners and residents lived in fear of their new neighbors and had already been nagging my dad to have his guys look out for their places. He just decided to make money doing it.

There were hundreds of salons, bars, liquor stores, drug stores, mini-marts, and apartment buildings in the North End and Dad had his guys visit all of them, guaranteeing the properties in question would be safe if they paid a weekly fee to Dad's organization. Geno was going to use his influence to go into the protection business. And his men could honestly make this guarantee—Willie was on the payroll as well and he made sure the word got out to his own clients whose businesses were protected.

Once again, everyone relaxed, knowing their neighborhood was safe and my dad turned this evolving situation into an opportunity to make money and this racket lasted for quite a while.

I know for a few years those two cleaned up in the area and the club and the Little Casino were the hot spots!

But this honeymoon period didn't last longer than those couple of years and the harmony and goodwill broke down with the locals and that area changed forever.

While Geno's revenue stream was growing rapidly, pressure was building in the North End, despite his attempt to maintain a sense of security. Change was in the air and blinded by the money he was making, he failed to see the bigger picture these modern times were ushering in.

My mom noticed this change, however. She saw how the neighborhood was reacting to Willie's club as well as the small but persistent tide of Black folks moving in, and she knew far better than my father that most people still viewed this new influx as a threat. Rena knew at some point the tension in the neighborhood was going to explode and she wanted to be far away when it did.

It was then she decided she wanted a home in the suburbs and once she latched onto an idea, she was as tenacious as a pit bull and there was no changing her mind. When I look back at it now, I don't think either she or my father realized what a life altering change; this decision to move -- which would be simple for most people, would mean for our family. To make matters worse, from my dad's point of view, she would use any fuel that came her way to bolster her position and as luck would have it for her, Dangling Man entered our life.

I barely remember the incident, but the story goes like this.

It was around ten or eleven in the evening on a late summer night and my parents, and I were home watching our giant black and white TV. We could hear a fight down the street close to Willie's place, but this wasn't unusual. Fights between Blacks and whites happened almost every night Willie's club was open although my dad's guys were usually able to quickly squelch them. But that night, there was more of a ruckus than usual, and you could just feel the tension in the air.

The phone rang and my mom went into the kitchen to answer it. It wasn't unusual for us to get late night phone calls, business at the Little Casino was in full swing at that hour, and so it happened frequently.

"Hello□" she said.

"Oh, hi, Willie. What's going on? I can barely hear you."

She listened to Willie speak as my dad made his way into the kitchen.

"Oh, Willie, that's terrible. Hold on. Here he is. Bye."

"Some kind of problem with the club," she said to my dad as she covered the receiver with her hand and passed the phone to him.

"Hey, Willie, I hear you got a problem. What's up□" said my dad, taking the phone.

He did nothing but listen for a couple of minutes, except to occasionally make a little grunt to indicate he was still on the line while Willie explained whatever problem it was he was having.

"Calm down. I'll send a couple of guys over now and I'll take care of the rest of it in the morning. Try to stay cool the rest of the night."

My mom was less than thrilled to hear this for sure, but it was more fuel for her argument to move so she tucked that into her mental arsenal. She had just been preaching earlier that evening about how bad the area was getting and how she just wanted to live in a peaceful, quiet neighborhood where everyone got along. Blacks, whites, Asians, whoever lived there.

Mom and dad came back into the living room but before I fell asleep in front of the TV, I heard him say to her, "Those stupid Guineas who've been giving my guys a hard time the past couple of days are over at Willie's causing some trouble. I'll send a few more guys over now to keep an eye on things and in the morning, the Rizzos will pay them a visit."

"Don't worry, Rena. Everything will be fine."

The next thing I knew, a loud crash woke me up as I slept in my bed. In an instant, my mom opened the door to my bedroom and said, "Kevin, stay right there. Do NOT leave your bed," and closed the door.

If you know me today, you know I never like being told what to do. I was even worse as a spoiled child. So, I immediately got out of bed and peeked out of my room, almost getting crushed by a couple of dad's guys flying past me to the back porch.

I heard my mom yell to them, "He's outside. Come quick!"

Then I head another voice on the porch yelling, "Whitey, don't do it," while someone else was yelling, "we'll take care of him!"

By this time, the entire building was awake. I took advantage of the confusion to sneak into the kitchen. Several men, plus Shirley and Dotty were there, joining my mother. They all had panicked looks on their faces.

My mom was on the phone, and I heard her say, "Thanks, Sonny. See you in a minute," before she hung up. She started to cry, and Shirley led her into the living room.

Outside on the porch, I could hear my dad, as mad as I've ever heard him yelling, "You stupid fucking niggers. Do you KNOW who you're screwing with? You are one DEAD son of a bitch!"

Some of the guys on the porch were yelling to my dad, "No, Whitey, no, no!"

No one was paying attention to me, and I had to know what the commotion was all about, so I snuck over to peek out the kitchen window.

What I saw was my dad in his underwear, dangling a Black guy over the railing of our third-floor porch. My dad had one of his hands around this petrified guy's throat and another one around his ankle as he began to lower him to drop him to the pavement below.

The guys on the porch inched closer to my father, continuing to say, "No, Whitey, no! Don't do it!" as my father screamed, "This is one dead, stupid nigger!"

Just then, the kitchen floor began to shake as all three hundred pounds of Sonny burst into the room like a galloping Clydesdale and everyone got Hell out of the way.

I will never forget the look on Sonny's face. There was a serious look written across his face, like he was chasing down a quarterback.

The room got quiet, and everything stopped as Sonny made it to the porch. If Sonny couldn't stop my dad from killing this guy, no one could. If he failed, this guy would go over the rail and hit the pavement three stories below.

"Whitey," he said to my dad. "Let me handle this. I'll take care of it. You shouldn't be getting your hands dirty." "Getting your hands dirty" was gangster speak for, "You're too important to be killing anybody and risk going to jail."

A calm came over my dad's face as if he had just seen a manifestation of the Virgin Mary. He was still holding the guy by the throat, but he nodded "okay" to Sonny and Sonny and two other guys grabbed the guy from my dad. I can't tell you how long this all took -- it seemed like hours -- although it was probably just a few seconds.

My dad walked into his bedroom, put some pants on and came back out. There was such chaos it wasn't until just then Dotty noticed I had seen the entire scene unfold. She led me back to bed, tucked me in and stayed with me until I fell asleep. But I could hear Sonny and a couple of the boys dragging this guy down the porch stairs. When I say "dragging," I mean you could hear his head and body bouncing off the wooden steps and eventually on to the sidewalk which at least he hadn't been dropped on.

The four of them disappeared into the night and everything calmed down, although the house was full of people pretty much all night long. Mom had pots of coffee going and one of the guys ran out and picked up bags of doughnuts from somewhere.

The next morning, I woke up to my parents arguing about moving out of the city. Apparently, while Mom wanted out before, this incident triggered her to want to be out for sure.

Now.

That was the final impetus for our moving to the suburbs, which happened just under two years later.

Many years later, I learned the backstory of "Dangling Man."

Dangling Man had been at Willie's that night, getting stupid drunk and he started bitching about how ineffective my dad and his gang had been about handling some of the white riffraff. Fortified with liquid courage, he and a couple of his buddies went up the back porch stairs to our apartment with the idea of confronting my father about this.

It was no problem for him to enter, for like I said, no one ever locked their doors, but he stumbled when he entered our kitchen and knocked over a chair. Hearing this, Dangling Man's buddies ran like hell down the stairs and left him alone to deal with my dad who flew out of the bedroom, dragged him out to the porch and prepared to throw him over the railing.

Two of my dad's guys across the street saw the Dangling Man's other two accomplices run out of our apartment building. There was always someone watching our building; every night some of the lower-level guys would get that shitty job. They called into the casino for back up and ran across the street up to our apartment. Their quick arrival saved Dangling Man's life for sure as my dad was about to toss him onto the pavement from three stories up. Someone uninvited (especially a Black man) entering the house was something that infuriated my dad beyond all reason.

As mad as my dad was, my mom was livid.

I know at least two meetings happened the next day. One consisted of the Rizzo brothers taking care of Dangling Man's cohorts and my dad visiting Willie to fix another.

From that night on, Willie always had one of his guys posted outside our building and Dad had two guys watching the luncheonette. My dad also put two of his guys on street patrol around the neighborhood every night of the week.

I can tell you no one ever entered our building again unless they were supposed to be there. There was one time I saw someone get jacked up trying to get into the building. My uncle Kenny (my mom's brother) paid a surprise visit from Maine. He made it to the first step before he was dragged off the steps and slammed against the building before things got cleared up. Our human powered building protection system worked better than any manufacturer's security alarm system.

I only heard the Dangling Man story a couple of times because just thinking about it, even years later, really pissed my mom off.

I never knew what happened to Dangling Man or his buddies. But once Sonny said he would take care of something, it was really taken care of, and he had Rizzo's to help. Dad never had to worry about anything Sonny oversaw, as he and my dad thought exactly alike. Problems always went away when Sonny was responsible for resolving them.

It was at that time that I got my first dog, a German shepherd named Jinx. I was thrilled to have a pet and my dad thought having a guard dog around would calm my mom down. The last thing he needed or wanted was my mom nagging him about moving daily, but it was too late for that. My mom started to hint she would leave him if he didn't move us soon and now, she had The Dangling Man to use against him.

5. HOLIDAY IN THE SUNSHINE STATE

The Dangling Man incident continued to affect our family long after it had been resolved. My mother was more intent than ever (if that was possible) to move to the suburbs and my dad was at his wits end to both appease her and continue his operations.

His solution was to take us on a family vacation to Florida, which, as far as he was concerned, was a two-fold win.

Even though he wouldn't admit it to anyone at first, not even my mom, he had resigned himself to moving out of his kingdom and into the suburbs, but he was a "cash only" kind of a guy and even though we were quite comfortable, buying a house was going to require a lot more cash on hand than usual.

To that end, he decided to buy Greyhounds, so he set up a meeting with a dog racing syndicate in Miami. My dad already owned a couple racing thoroughbred horses, so owning greyhounds was just a natural progression.

You see, owning racing dogs and horses is an extremely expensive proposition, even if they are often running in fixed races. There is training, room and board and travel expenses. From the time I was born until right before his death, Geno usually owned two dogs and two horses at a time. The expenses for these animals were thousands of dollars a month so it was important they earned their keep.

Mom wasn't thrilled about this expansion into yet another expensive area of organized crime, but she went along with it to get some time in the sun and sand.

Clearly, there were a few inherent flaws to this Florida road trip, but this "time out" for my mother turned out to be more stressful than if we had just stayed at home.

I was excited about going to the beach in Florida, too. If you know anything about Hartford, Connecticut, beaches are in short supply around there.

What I didn't count on was the hours and hours of being in the back seat of our giant green Cadillac while my father drove south. As anyone who has ever been a little kid in similar circumstances knows, these hours felt like years. But Geno was good about stopping a lot along the way to keep me quiet and happy. On our "pit stops" he would give Mom a wad of cash so she could buy her and me whatever we wanted and while we were taking in the sights, shopping, and getting ice cream, he'd make calls to Hartford to check on things up there and would also call Miami to firm up his business arrangements there.

As soon as we got to Miami, he dropped Mom and me off at our motel and scurried off to meet with other like-minded gangsters. They all shared an interest in making alliances on the dog track circuit, primarily by buying and selling dogs.

That week, Mom and I spent most of our time on the beach, although we visited my dad at the track a couple of times. I loved dogs and wanted to see the ones Dad was thinking about buying although my mother had already explained to me that just like the horses he owned, they wouldn't be living at home in Hartford with us.

One day we went to the track with him.

My parents set up a rendezvous point for a few hours later before he gave Mom another roll of cash, the car keys and disappeared into the crowd to work his deals. My mom and I jumped into the Cadillac and took off. We went shopping, ate lunch and just generally had a fun time. When we were done, we made it back to the meeting point at the agreed upon time and waited and waited but Geno was a no show.

Mom was getting pissed and had him paged across the track. Even though she was upset, I got quite a kick out of hearing "DiBacco" coming out of all the loudspeakers.

We waited for quite a while longer, but he finally emerged from the press box area with a fist full of papers. He had just purchased two of the area's best Greyhounds and he was in a great mood, although when Mom asked him what this venture cost us, he whispered in her ear, and she just rolled her eyes. She clearly wasn't sharing his enthusiasm.

Nonetheless, we piled into the Cadillac and went to a fancy steak house to celebrate. After a couple of drinks, Manhattans for them and a Roy Rogers for me, the mood loosened, and we were all laughing. Mom shoveled down scallops and lobster, Dad had a huge steak and I had one of my favorite meals, a hot dog and fries.

It was a nice ending to the day, and we were exhausted by the time we got back to the motel. As Mom and I got ready for bed, Dad promised us a family day at the beach in the morning before he went outside to call Sonny.

I went to sleep extremely excited.

We were up early the next day. Dad was packing ice into a cooler and Mom was getting the beach gear together: blankets, towels, toys, books, and lotions even though the beach was literally thirty feet from our motel. We could just walk up the path from the water to our room in less than a minute if we needed anything or forgot something.

But for some reason, my parents were packing the Cadillac to go somewhere.

We were going to the beach all right. Just not the public beach right next to us.

Dad's associates had given him access to their own private beach resort and he planned on taking full advantage of it.

So, we finished packing up the Cadillac and headed out on the short trip over there. We went up a long, white pebble and seashell paved driveway lined with tall palm trees laden with bunches of coconuts.

I knew this place was a big deal as soon as we got to the guard house and gate and were met by a couple of guys wearing shorts, matching bowling shirts and name tags. Both called my dad "Sir." After we pulled in and the gates closed behind us, they put a card on his dashboard and showed him where to park, pointing to several cars in a nearby parking lot. I kept asking why there were so many cars like ours there, but I couldn't get an answer to this question.

We parked in front of a glass house on the beach. A Latino looking guy who was also wearing one of those bowling shirts and a name tag greeted us and there were other men wearing the same uniform walking around, setting up beach furniture, getting drinks and other stuff like that. I smiled at one of them who handed me some candy.

Dad opened the trunk, and these name-tagged guys carried all our blankets, the cooler, and our other gear to a beach area behind the glass house. Right before the beach was a recreation area which had a small, pristine light blue pool surrounded by deck chairs and small tables, a cement shuffleboard table and an outside bar that already had stools and big umbrellas set up and music playing.

There was no one near us for what seemed like a hundred yards and the staff set everything up. We had the largest beach umbrella I had ever seen with wide bright pink and white stripes, and they brought over a couple of chaise lounges made of tubular aluminum coils. The lounges had thin, wide slats which were covered by thick, plastic covered cushions decorated with a pineapple and palm tree themed print trimmed with short white fringe. They even brought me my own chair that matched the chaise lounges, but it had a slider and its own little awning, and I thought that was very cool.

As usual, Geno gave them a nice tip. My father always tipped the help no matter how small of a job they did. One of the staff took our order and went to the bar to get drinks for my parents and a grape Nehi for me while we settled in.

My dad didn't have much to do to get comfortable. He was already wearing what passed as beach attire in his mind. Knee length pale yellow board shorts with thin maroon stripes. Its waistband barely covered his potbelly, and the rest of the fabric did a mediocre job of covering his pale white legs. He also wore a brightly colored, cotton, button down Hawaiian print shirt Mom had picked up for him on one of our many shopping excursions on the way down. Black socks which stopped a few inches below his knees and a pair of tan straw huarache sandals completed his ensemble. The only work he had to do was to claim one of the lounges and make sure it was well under the umbrella. He hated being in the direct sun.

For her part, Mom took off the long linen beach dress and sandals she had been wearing and revealed the black, pleated one-piece bathing suit with a wide silver zipper up the back she had underneath it. She put on a giant black straw beach hat, lathered herself with baby oil— "Helps you tan faster," she told me as she put some on me as well—and looking like the stunning beach beauty she was, she took her place in the sun on the other lounge.

While I was extremely excited about having my own chair, one that rocked back and forth over the sand no less, I walked down to the edge of the water and waded out a bit before Mom called me back to her, promising me we would go for a swim after we had our drinks. I obeyed her of course and went back to my blanket in the sun and happily began making sandcastles and moats.

The last thing I remember before a panicked waitress loudly woke the three of us up was filling my moat with water.

Apparently, we all had fallen asleep, Dad in the shade and Mom and I in the direct sun. The waitress was yelling over to the other workers and the lifeguard. My dad woke up to the commotion to discover my mom and I were lobster red.

The workers draped Mom and I in blankets and moments later an ambulance arrived to take us to the hospital. I had suffered third degree sunburn on my back and neck and was vomiting and crying in pain. My mom had second-degree burns and the emergency workers dressed them before we started in route to the hospital while Dad followed behind us in the Cadillac.

I went in and out of consciousness and ended up being sedated for the pain. I was admitted to the hospital and placed into the ICU. I stayed in the hospital for three days, part of which was in a medically induced coma because of my excruciating pain.

I obviously don't remember much about this event. But I do know my dilemma was a common problem Floridians had seen many times -- Yankees not knowing when to get out of the sun.

The entire vacation mood had changed and now my parents just wanted to go home. Dad called our family doctor, Dr. Gerwitz, back home in Hartford to get his opinion. Dr Gerwitz to see if he agreed with Florida doctors, or wanted to change, the treatments that the Florida doctors recommended. After my three days in the hospital, we stayed one more day at the motel before we began heading back north.

I was weak and on some serious painkillers. What had started out to be a fun business trip and vacation ended up depressing my mom. It was supposed to be a relaxing time; it was anything but. My dad ended up purchasing his racing dogs, so he was happy even though this leg of the trip had become costly.

We had no idea this was just the beginning of the expensive misadventures which became part of our Florida "vacation" as we started the journey North.

The Florida trip was not exactly going as planned, especially as far as my mother and I were concerned. So, Dad decided to make up for it, in another one of his own warped win-win ways. The win for him was we were going to take the scenic journey home from Florida. When I say the "scenic journey," I mean his plan was to stop at all the major horse racetracks between Florida and Connecticut. How he thought this would be relaxing for Mom and me who were still recovering from our sunburns, I don't know.

But he wasn't a total jerk. As we prepared to head back North, he told us he would agree to move to the suburbs and buy us a nice house. He also explained that to pay for this venture, he needed to increase his earnings at the tracks.

When he announced this, Mom immediately figured out the scam he had been running the entire time we had been on the road and "on vacation." His horses had been making the same circuit, at the same time as our road trip. She quickly realized this little" vacation" had been planned well ahead of time, part of the reason my dad was constantly looking for pay phones both while we were on the road and in Florida. Although she hated his manipulations, she succumbed to them, assuming he was doing all he could to raise enough money for her house. Apparently betting on horses and dogs wasn't much of a gamble for my dad as his connections fixed most of the races at tracks up and down the East Coast either with ringer horses, paid off jockeys or doping horses.

Our first stop on our trip heading back North was Fort Lauderdale where I spent another week recovering. Through some miracle, this break in our travels turned out to be another win-win for the four of us.

Yes, the four of us.

In Fort Lauderdale we added a new member to our entourage, my mom's friend Shirley.

My parents had met Shirley years before on one of their many trips to Florida. She was a stunning Italian/Cuban beauty queen and was a hostess at one of their favorite clubs down there when their paths first crossed. On top of being beautiful, she was smart and vivacious, and she and my mom hit it off right away and my dad liked her as well. He thought she would be a great friend and companion for my mom. Even though she lived far away from Barbour Street, Shirley and my mom talked on the phone all the time, so they were always up to date on what was going on in each other's lives. When we stopped by to see her, Shirley already knew about my mother's increasing dissatisfaction with our lives in Hartford and my mom knew Shirley's marriage was going sour but none of us had any idea how terrible things were for her until we got there.

During dinner on one of our first nights there, Shirley broke down and with tears in her eyes and her voice quivering, she told my parents the truth.

Norman, her husband, had hit her during a recent argument they had had and while she wanted to leave him, she had nowhere to go. All her family was still in Cuba, and she didn't want to return there but she didn't have any Floridian friends to turn to for help.

My parents were shocked to learn this and even my dad was very sympathetic. Geno had more bad qualities than most people but being a wife beater was not one of them. It was probably the only moral he had. He would not tolerate any woman being hit. Looking back one of the few lessons he taught me was to never hit a woman. Only cowards hit females. I followed that rule all my life.

After I had been tucked into bed that night, I fell asleep listening to them discuss how best to help her. It was my dad's idea to bring Shirley with us back to Connecticut. To not only get her out of this terrible situation but to also have her around to be company for my mom. Shirley was offered a place to live in our building on Barbour Street.

It was the perfect solution for her terrible situation.

Rena loved this idea immediately and over the next couple of days she convinced Shirley to leave "Norman the

Bum" and come back to Connecticut with us to start a new life. Shirley was sold on the idea.

Mom helped her discreetly pack a few personal belongings and the day we left Fort Lauderdale; we picked her up and brought her back to our motel so she could help my mom pack our things while my dad had one last errand to attend to.

I remember two guys in a big blue Cadillac pulled up to the motel to pick him up and he immediately jumped into the front seat. Shirley was crying as they drove away, and my mom tried to comfort her. She told Shirley she was going to be just fine with us and that once we got back to Connecticut she could file for divorce and be done with Norman.

Obviously, the three of us weren't around when Dad and his friends paid Norman a visit. But I do know they gave him a warning which didn't involve a lot of talking. I always believed he received a merciless beating and only lived because Shirley wanted it that way.

That incident was never mentioned again, nor was his name.

The four of us continued our journey back North to our little Barbour Street compound. Dad wanted to keep to his plan to stop at the racetrack and so we did. We made side trips to all the important tracks in West Virginia, Maryland, Delaware, and New Jersey as we edged our way up the East Coast. If it was a business (race) day, he would leave us the car and plenty of cash and he would come back to the motel and take us all out for a fancy dinner where we were often joined by trainers, jockeys, and some of his other business associates. Some nights there would be as many as ten other people with us. Everyone at these dinners was incredibly happy and that could only mean one thing.

Dad was making money with his horses by winning fixed races.

Mom was happy about this because the more money he made, even though she was less than thrilled about his methodology, the closer she was to getting to her house. And she loved having Shirley with us. Shirley was good company for her during the long legs driving and a welcome addition to the formerly "all men" business dinners. She also picked up the slack entertaining me when Rena wanted to take a nap or just have a couple of hours to herself.

For her part, Shirley was thrilled to be getting further and further away from slimy Norman who could never hurt her again. She had known my parents long enough to know they would (and did) keep their promise to keep her safe and not wanting anything.

As for me, my sunburn eventually dissipated on our meandering trip home.

I learned a lot of geography. I remember riding through the different states and Shirley and my mom quizzing me on the state capitals and license plate colors. Shirley became my mother number two. On that trip I simply adored her, and her personality meshed with my mom. When we stopped for the day or to take a break, Dad would make his phone calls or go to the track and the three of us would go shopping, to a beach or playground or out for ice cream. I had a ball!

That back trip was win-win-win-win in a brand-new Cadillac filled with happy campers until we made out last stop before we got home. This stop was at the world-famous Belmont horse track in New York, home of the final leg of the Triple Crown.

There are some gaps in my memory about this next incident, the reasons for which will shortly become evident.

I'm not sure what day it was, not that it matters much, but I know it was on a weekend.

As my mother told me the story, Shirley and I had fallen asleep in our Cadillac's huge back seat, long before we pulled into the Belmont area. I woke up on the floor with Shirley pulling me back up on the seat. My mom was kneeling over her seat in the front, checking to see if I was okay. Dad was screaming at the top of his lungs to someone in a vehicle behind us. I was sleepy and very confused.

I quickly learned some drunken pinhead in a Buick truck (a lesser vehicle than a Cadillac if ever there was one) had rear-ended us at a traffic light just outside of the track. The damage to our car was minimal. In those days, cars were steel and had huge chrome bumpers. It would have taken a major impact to do any real damage to the Cadillac and fortunately, this was not the case.

But that didn't stop my father from being raving mad. He jumped out of our car and was ready to decapitate the other driver when a policeman in a bubble top cruiser arrived on the scene. The officer somehow managed to calm my father down, which by now you know was surely not an easy task, arrested the guy and took him off to jail. Before he left, he had the truck towed and gave all the owner's information to my father.

Despite all this commotion, we made it inside the track just in time to see Dad's horses run. They finished first and second as usual. We left the track, but before heading to our motel for the night, we went to the police station where my dad filed a report. He had already called his lawyer who had quickly filed both a lawsuit and criminal charges.

I remember my parents saying the drunk was going to pay dearly, but more importantly to me, the motel had a nice pool and an excellent restaurant nearby.

The next morning, the grownups decided to stay near the track one more day so Dad could watch his horses run on their last day there. Mom dropped him off at the track in our now dented Cadillac and then she, Shirley and I headed out for our final day of road trip shopping and eating. I never get tired of eating, but I can't say I was sorry to see my days of shopping come to an end.

It was going to be a simple, fun day and as far as I was concerned, it was. Dad had his races fixed, so for him it was just the thrill of being on the track when they ran.

Our simple fun day ended when we got back to the track.

We had owner's passes and could wander anywhere we pleased except for the inspection area where officials check the horses and do the end of the day race weighing on the jockeys. The three of us went to the stalls in the stables where our horses were to find my dad. It was then we learned he had had a two-day bad streak. Yesterday's accident had now been surpassed by today's incident when his "winning horse" finished in the middle of the pack.

A jockey who had always been one of his favorites and was supposed to throw the race had a sudden change of heart and screwed my dad over. All the other jockeys he had paid off had done their jobs, but this con artist cost my dad thousands of dollars.

We quickly left my dad who was heading to the locker room to find this jockey and the three of us went up to the grandstand restaurant where Mom and Shirley had a few drinks. Even though I was just a little boy, I knew life was about to get exceedingly difficult for this four-foot jockey who had decided to disobey 'the fix.'

My father and the attendant waited outside of the locker room for this deadbeat jockey to leave. Finally, Geno got impatient and went in with the attendant to look for this little guy. By now, most of the jockeys were leaving the locker room. As they exited, Dad pulled his other jockey contacts aside to ask where this chooch was. Most of them were deathly afraid to say or do anything wrong as they just got a week's pay from my dad and didn't want to further upset him and a couple of them went back into the locker room to try and find this other jockey. Apparently, he had waited until the last turn to have his official outgoing inspection. This area was the only place on the entire track my dad was not allowed.

When the other jockeys told my father how this guy was stalling, he was even more furious. It wasn't until a couple of hours later he found out the jockey had slipped out of the official's area through the back door and snuck out of the track.

Unbeknownst to my dad, this was also about the time my mom and Shirley had had enough of waiting themselves and we all went down trackside to find him. By now it was dark, and my father was furious. He told a few of the trainers still at the track he would be looking for this "rat" jockey. My mom had to calm him down and somehow got us all to a local Italian restaurant where he could unwind and feel comfortable. The grownups all ordered drinks and a soda for me, and Geno eventually calmed down. He had two beautiful women by his side; what guy wouldn't like that? My dad's temper could go from zero to a hundred and back down in a second and it was my mom who usually knew how to handle this type of situation.

What had taken place was something gangsters do not take lightly; Geno had been swindled. On top of that, his horse made no money on that race and the entire scheme ended up costing him dearly. That was the first and only time that kind of double cross ever happened, as I recall. From then on, my father had a "middleman" at each race to make sure his plans went off without a hitch. The middleman was always a big, tough guy who ensured that everyone who had been paid off: the jockey, track owner and someone in the racing commission (since this was regulated by the state) played their role. I never heard of any trouble at any track from that point on and I'm not sure what happened to the jockey. Once my father god that mad there was no telling what he would do. I'm very sure it didn't end well for the little guy.

I was always nosing around my dad's conversations, listening in like some sort of kid spy. But I was too young to understand exactly what he did.

I knew he owned a restaurant; I was there all the time.

I knew he had parties in the restaurant's basement and on the first floor of our building.

I knew there were always the same people around me.

I knew he owned horses and Greyhounds. They weren't my pets even though I got to visit them at their stables or kennels now and then. Like every kid with a cowboy obsession, I loved horses and sometimes they'd take me to the country for a pony ride. Not content with that, I started riding lessons and they promised I could get my own horse if I stuck with my lessons but riding a horse for real was much harder than it looked on TV and my interest in becoming a real cowboy with my own horse quickly faded.

I did not know what this all meant. I just thought it was part of a normal Italian childhood.

6. COMMENCE MISSION: OPERATION HOUSE DETOUR: MAINE

In gambling terms, while my dad didn't completely beat the house, he was certainly still ahead of the game when we returned to Barbour Street after our road holiday trip. Even with a dented Cadillac and his last day loss at Belmont, he still had his two new Greyhounds and had won all his other races. Sonny and the rest of the Gabardine Gang had done their job and kept his other operations running smoothly and making money while we were away, so everything on that front was business as usual. Things had even been calm at Willie's!

Dad was thrilled to be back home and in control of our neighborhood. He loved working at Pal's and the Little Casino and always enjoyed his club nights with the guys over at Willie's. While he often groused about the pressure my mother put on him to buy us a house within a year under no uncertain terms, I initially thought he somewhat liked the challenge of kicking things up another notch. To that end, he spent long hours with the rest of the Gabardine Gang discussing their best options for increasing their revenue streams to meet this new goal and he helped my mom get Shirley settled in.

Charlie, who lived across the hall from us and was supposed to help my dad with maintenance on his properties, he had always been more of a bother than he was worth overall, so my dad talked his daughter into taking him in to live with her. Shirley, for her part, stayed with us until he moved out, a month or so later. She made a nice comfortable home for him on the other side of Hartford. He was close enough where he could visit my dad when he wanted. During that time, Shirley and my mom went shopping for furniture for her new apartment. Just about every day and when they weren't shopping, Mom was making curtains and doing other things for her to help her get adjusted to a new city. Once she was settled in, she joined the family business, taking waitressing shifts at the luncheonette and as a hostess at the Little Casino. Everyone loved her and she got great tips from all the customers.

I was happy to be back home in a familiar neighborhood with familiar faces. My nanny Dotty was excited to have me back under her wing. I was like the child she never had. I was happy to be back in my usual routine. As much as I loved my mom, I had missed Dotty a lot on our road trip. We had developed a different type of bond, more like a brother sister dynamic.

I didn't know what my parents were planning, nor did I care. The only thing I knew was Mom kept telling me soon I would have my own yard and friends my own age in a safe, small town away from the city. I was extremely excited about this, and this made my mother happy and increasingly confident about her decision.

By the beginning of the year, Geno was ready to begin the big push to save enough money to buy a house. My mom was getting tired of the city and the noise. With the help of one of my dad's connections, Mom started a full-time job as a supervisor in a finalizing department at the Gold Leaf Company. This company would powderize gold from real gold bars and turn it into thin gold strips for fancy labels and other decorative things. Once my mother started there, Shirley picked up a lot of the jobs my mother had always done for my dad's business; mostly keeping up with supplies needed for Pal's, the Little Casino, and the Clubhouse but she also kept most of her waitress and hostessing shifts.

Dad really worked at increasing the volume of all his businesses and succeeded at that. But more people and more company projects meant he was out until dawn nearly every night. As for hijacking more trucks, that was easy enough. There was never a shortage of merchandise-laden trailers and boxcars going through Hartford. His contacts in the police department ensured he always knew when and what valuable cargo was going through town and being who he was, he never had a shortage of men willing to make a week's pay for just a couple of hours of occasional, low-risk, tax free work.

This boom in stolen clothing and accessories also helped with his and Willie's prostitution businesses. An increase in merchandise meant they were able to attract more beautiful women to work for them and those women spent more money on clothing, furs, and jewelry. In turn, this meant the girls started attracting a more affluent clientele who would then spend money gambling at my dad's places and on drinks at Willie's to impress them. This revenue stream didn't turn into a river overnight by any means, but it certainly didn't take long for it to grow into a nice steady flow.

My mother was not a high maintenance kind of a woman, nor was she prissy. She was confident about her looks and, more importantly, her abilities. But it became clear after a while the constant stream of gorgeous "working girls" always around the apartment, club and restaurant was starting to grate on her. My parents began to fight more. It wasn't the women, or the game-room got under my mom' skin, it was the fact that my father was setting up illegal abortion clinics. More than anything else this gave her a bad feeling. The tension was evident, and the arguments started becoming more frequent.

The clinics were just another way to make money. My mom was not happy with this concept at all.

He set up two abortion clinics in Hartford and collaborated with a couple of shady doctors. The purpose of these clinics and doctors was to provide illegal abortions for women who needed them.

I know this is vastly different from what you've seen and read about the Mafia disapproving abortions for religious and moral reasons, but that was not the case at all. It wasn't a matter of morality for these organizations. The "big organizations" you've always heard about simply didn't waste their time on such small chunks of money, but that kind of money was huge for small crime guys like my dad and his gang.

Remember, not only was abortion illegal then, but it was often performed with crude procedures by people with little or no medical training and sometimes a literal back alley for an operating room. The marketplace in my dad's sphere of influence was more than receptive to this service, and a real doctor with a basement office near a hospital in case there was a problem (in case something went terribly wrong and often it did) was at least a step up from an alleyway. Not only was being unmarried and pregnant taboo, but with my father's line of work in the prostitution business, he frequently ran into women for whom this was a professional hazard. He literally could control, and make money off, the entire process. There was one doctor who did procedures on woman ages thirteen to fifty, so age wasn't an issue. Black, White, Asian, it didn't matter. My dad's goons would even pick the women up in the nice Cadillacs, bring them to the clinic and drop them back off at home.

Nothing mattered just as long as they could pay and pay with cash.

This business was the one that drove my mother to the brink. My mom was incensed that my dad had gotten involved in this activity and "started playing with people's lives," as she called it. When my father refused to stop this, she got so angry she called Grandpa Don, packed her and me up and we went off to live with her parents in Maine (where she grew up) for the summer.

I didn't know this was a separation. I didn't even know what marital separation was. I only knew that Mom was taking some time off from her job and Dad was doing his business as usual in Hartford. Grandma and Grandpa drove down from Maine to pick Mom and me up. I was extremely excited at the prospect of being in the woods next to Moosehead Lake all summer and their huge family camp there was not a disappointment.

A paper mill in a small town near the lake drove the local economy. The mill had bought all the land around the lake as back then, proximity to lakes and more importantly, the rivers that feed them, were critical to the paper business. The mill was on one side of Moosehead Lake, and it would lease the land around the lake to its employees at ten or twenty-year increments and in turn the workers would get lake front property, cheap land, and discounted lumber. It was a perfect arrangement for my grandfather and uncles who were lifelong mill workers and they all got land near each other. My grandparents' camp had a small guesthouse they fixed up for Mom and me to stay in. It had no electricity and no indoor bathroom, and so I had my introduction to the good ol' "Maine Outhouse."

Time flies when you're a kid and my summer in Maine was no exception.

I spent my days fishing for trout with Grandpa Don (although we usually just caught perch or an occasional pickerel) and swimming in icy Moosehead Lake. On top of that, the campsite always had radio or records on, and the air was filled with music and conversation over card games and cooking.

There was always a lot of cooking and eating going on. My mom's family knew how to eat and drink, that's for sure. The food my aunts made daily was incredible. We are talking about homemade Maine cooking with meat pies, lobsters, shrimps, beefs stews, cookies cakes and pies, every day. I've said, my mom was no slouch in the cooking department either, now I know where she learned it. These weren't the healthiest meals to eat. Everything was made with heavy cream, sugar, and fat but it sure was good!

My dad and Shirley stayed in Connecticut. Dad was doing business as usual, and Shirley had fallen in love with a guy named David. Mom had begged her to come to Maine with us, but she wanted to stay behind with her new beau. She promised to look after my dad and keep him out of trouble. My dad, for his part, gave David and his brother jobs acquiring and moving stolen goods.

Mom's family camp started to break down around Labor Day. Everyone was packing up to go to their "regular" houses, except for my grandmother or "Mumma" as we called her. Even though she and my grandfather had a house closer to the mill, she loved being alone against the elements. The rest of the family, including Grandpa Don, was totally okay with that and when I look back on it, I think they all secretly rooted for the elements.

Mumma was the toughest old bird I've ever met and that's saying something considering I grew up surrounded by tough, mean people. She had a thick Maine accent along with linebacker shoulders from chopping wood all summer and muscular legs from snowshoeing all winter. Mumma was the strongest woman I ever met. She looked more like a female Russian weightlifter than a grandmother, that's for sure! She would hunt moose, deer and even bears. Remember Grandpa Don? He was one of the five husbands she married and divorced; I don't quite remember where he fell in that order. Mumma had no fear and many times she chased her cheating husbands out the door with her shotgun.

As we were packing up the Cadillac, Mumma took Dad aside and said, "Hey, Geno, I want a word in private with you before you guys hit the road. Now seems like a good time. Come, take a walk with me."

"Rena, you and Kev take one last look in the cabin and make sure you haven't forgotten anything, especially you,

Kev. I don't want you calling and crying you left a cowboy boot or some other nonsense here."

"Good idea, Ma," my mom said, catching my dad's eye and shrugging her shoulders a little. "Just don't keep him too long! I want to get on the road before the traffic gets bad."

"Sure Mumma, anything for you," my dad said to Grandma without an ounce of sincerity.

"It'll just take a minute," Mumma said, adjusting the hunting rifle she always had with her at dawn so she could shoot whatever was in season. She started down the driveway heading away from camp and my father had no choice but to follow her.

My entire childhood was spent being surrounded by the meanest, toughest people I have met. My own father was just as mean as Al Capone, but it was Mumma who scared me to death. Having just spent the summer with her and her temperament, I didn't have to have to hear a word of the conversation she was having with my dad, to know exactly what words were heading his way.

Everyone my father knew worked for him, did business with him or was his customer. If you weren't any of those things, more likely than not, you were smart, so that meant you were scared and stayed away from him. Mumma was neither a business associate nor scared. Even worse for my dad, she could read him like a book, and she didn't like the story line.

I couldn't hear the conversation of course, but I could see Mumma. Dad's back was to me. Her face was terribly angry and while she never exactly pointed her shotgun at him, she sure did gesture with it to make her point a couple of times. From seeing just this, even as a little boy I knew what was going on.

Mom had spoken to Mumma many times over the summer about how hard it had been to get Dad to pony up and buy her a house. Mumma didn't understand why he hadn't just bought her one the minute she mentioned it.

First, Mumma mentioned if he didn't make good on his promise to buy Mom and me a house and "Soon!" (and here's where the gesturing with the rifle comes in) she'd take a shotgun to his ass.

Then she casually remarked that unlike big cities, a body dumped in the Maine woods would probably never be found.

My father had a few things to consider during that discussion. They included her temper, her gun collection and her shooting ability.

He decided to take her warning to heart.

Once that summer ended, my dad had gained a newfound respect for her. I think he thought any old lady who would threaten to take out a gangster like him most likely would do it.

After that, I didn't want to visit Maine again because she was so mean and scary, although we continued to go for at least a couple of weeks every summer well into my teenage years. But when I got older, I began to understand on a deeply personal level the rationale behind my grandmother dealing with my father that day as she did.

7. MILK AND BREAD

Once again, our little family was on the road, intact and heading home to Barbour Street. At age five or six, I had logged more miles in a car than most adults have done in their entire lives so I'm a pretty good judge of what an uneventful ride is, and this was one of them. I could tell that my mother's and my summer in Maine had changed my dad's disposition somewhat although he was never one for soul searching.

Geno was the kind of guy who showed his love with gifts, fancy dinners, and trips but he wasn't one to say, "I love you." He certainly never said it to me and if he said it to my mom, I don't remember hearing it. However, I always believed our time away made him realize how much he really did love my mother. That, and my grandmother's threat to shoot him.

Whatever the reason, Dad was extra nice to Mom after this trip. She got more gifts than she knew what to do with and he helped her out running her end of things more than he usually did.

It only took a day or two for Mom to settle back in and get back up to speed with her usual routine. I think she had had enough of roughing it. By roughing it, I mean roughing it. There was no running water at the camp, you had to haul water up from the lake, there was no electricity, you cooked on a wood heated stove, an outhouse was the bathroom, and if you had to go to the store you would have to take the little motorboat across the lake.

She made sure Pal's, the Little Casino, and the Game Room were stocked exactly how she wanted them and made the rounds to all the vendors she regularly did business with just to say hi and let them know she was back in town. Everyone knew that my mom had spent the summer in Maine. They also knew that my mom was not happy with some of the decisions my dad made. She was back now and that's all they cared about. Rena was the light that lit up the room.

In a few weeks, everything was back to running to her satisfaction and she returned to her job at the Gold Leaf Company. The push for cash resumed more earnestly than ever after the gentle nudge from Momma and both my parents worked hard to put money away. They decided on the general area they wanted to move to and started looking at houses. Dad even started to occasionally bring up the topic of taking Mom on a real vacation, just the two of them, to Las Vegas. In addition, he made it a point to take her, Shirley, and David out to the club every Saturday night.

David turned out to be quite good at fencing "hot" property. He would just pull into a shopping center parking lot and sell whatever he had on hand out of the trunk of his car. He mostly had small stuff like radios and cameras that had been "confiscated" from stores and trucks; items Henry and the other David didn't have buyers for. He could turn these stolen items into quick cash for the organization in no time flat. Because he was Shirley's boyfriend, David was the only Black guy other than Sonny my father ever let into the organization and trusted with money. David and Sonny formed a nice team. They worked together well. My dad let them do their own thing and they were good at it. My dad trust Sonny like no other. Sonny had never disappointed my dad. If Sonny asked for anything, my dad was sure to give it to him with no questions asked. It was the love my dad had for Sonny that transferred over to all of us. At that youthful age I immediately recognized what real respect was.

It's almost impossible for me to say what an amazing influence Sonny had on me in my childhood. Most outsiders, and even most members of the gang, thought of him as nothing more than my dad's Black bodyguard and therefore just another gangster by virtue of that position.

But he was so much more than that to our family. We all loved Sonny, me, most of all, and he loved us as well. My mom used to say she had no doubt Sonny was Italian, just darker, and he and my dad were related somehow.

Even though he was constantly discriminated against, he was the nicest, warmest man I have ever met, and he was always smiling. I believe since I admired him so much, his influence had a major impact on my personality. He certainly is the focal point of one of the more unusual stories from my childhood.

Sonny's goal was to run his own operation one day, so one time, to show his appreciation and trust, my dad gave him a shot at managing a big job the gang was planning. Several boxcars full of brand new black and white Magnavox televisions were going to be arriving at the train station and Sonny was appointed the man in charge. This was an opportunity for Sonny to bring home some extra money to help his family. My dad was more than happy to let Sonny run this job.

It seemed like a safe job on paper. All he had to do was coordinate with the crew, set up the times the transportation and it would be a nice payday.

The security team at the station had already been paid off to be away from the tracks as the train pulled into the yard. In the shadows of a large parking lot, near the tracks and waiting for the train, were Sonny, the Rizzos, David and his brother and a couple dozen guys with about eight milk delivery trucks, which were about the same shape and size as mail delivery trucks.

The milk trucks used in this heist belong to a dairy owned by Italians who lived down state. Even though their business had gone belly up, they still owned a huge fleet of trucks. For a big percentage of the haul, they would provide as many vin and license plate numberless trucks as needed for a heist. Milk trucks were so common, no one thought twice about seeing one, even late at night because that was just the milk being delivered directly from the dairy, so it was at your doorstep first thing in the morning.

The plan was for the guys to load the TVs onto the milk trucks while the train made a scheduled stop. In turn, the trucks would be driven to buyers all around the state, their last stop being New Haven, where they were set on fire so they couldn't be traced.

The train pulled in and everything was going as planned. The station workers were on their break and my dad's guys were pros. It took them no time to unload the TVs off the boxcar and on to the milk trucks. But fate wasn't on their side that night.

They were almost done when an off-duty cop was driving by and couldn't help but notice the small fleet of milk trucks at the train station at two o'clock in the morning.

Had fate been kinder to Sonny and his crew by only five minutes at one end of the heist or the other, there would have been no problem.

The cop pulled over, spotted Sonny, approached him, and demanded to know what was going on. Realizing what he was seeing, the cop drew his gun and told Sonny to freeze.

Sonny shoved the cop and took off, but not before shots were fired. The policeman was hit in the shoulder and Sonny was shot in the stomach.

The cop ran to his patrol car to call for backup, but by then it was too late.

The milk trucks had hit the highway and scattered into the night.

David grabbed Sonny, threw him in the back of his Cadillac and drove him to my parents' apartment.

A commotion in our living room woke me up and I cracked open the door to see what was happening. The hallway door was open, and I could see Sonny lying there. David was kneeling over him, covered in blood, and holding a jacket on Sonny's stomach. Shirley had heard the noise and had already run over from across the hall and was standing in our living room. My dad was standing there too, disheveled and wearing nothing but his underwear. My mom was in the entranceway, crying hysterically.

"Rena, don't just stand there. Pull yourself together," my father yelled at her.

"Call the doc right away. Now!"

She flew past me to get to the phone in the kitchen. He quickly followed her there.

I inched out of my room and into the hallway to get a better view of what was going on.

On the kitchen table were eight or ten freshly baked loaves of bread and Dad grabbed several of them.

I had no idea why.

By then, Dotty had heard all the noise and had come up. Being a nursing student, she took over immediately.

"Towels," she yelled. "Towels!" and while my mother ran into the bathroom as quickly as she could to grab every towel she could get her hands on, my dad ran over to Dotty with all the loaves of bread he could carry in his arms.

"Use this," he yelled to Dotty. She looked at him puzzled as he ripped a loaf lengthwise and handed a half to her. She quickly understood what he meant, and she placed the bread over the bullet hole. The bread quickly absorbed the blood.

The bread was stopping the bleeding because the thick crust refused to let the blood out. Dad ripped another loaf in half and then another. Mom ran to them with a stack of towels and Dotty pulled off the bread.

The bleeding had stopped. My dad explained to the women it was an Old Italian fallback, just in case there weren't any towels around.

There was such chaos no one realized I was watching everything from the safety of my bedroom.

While the doctor was still in route, Sonny had no choice but to just take the pain, although Mom gave him a couple shots of whiskey in an attempt to help quell it.

Dr. Hertzberg arrived, bringing with him a friend of his who had been a media in the war and could patch anyone up in seconds. He instructed everyone to help move Sonny to the couch. It took four men and two women to get his 6'7," 340 pounds over there. He was in critical condition, but they couldn't take him to the hospital; the television heist was all over the news. The doctors had to do a M.A.S.H. surgery right there in the living room.

My mom was physically shaken and afraid, but when she finally noticed me, she quickly escorted me to bed. I'm sure I had seen more than my parents ever wanted me to.

I will never forget my dad's face before I was led away. He was more panicked than I had ever seen him, and it looked like he was going to cry.

I fell asleep quickly. I know for sure at some point my mother came into my room to check on me and lay down to get some rest herself for a few minutes. I know this because when I woke up to roll over, she was sleeping there next to me.

I woke up a few hours later and Mom had left my bedroom, but I could hear talking in the kitchen.

It was Mom and Dad, Shirley, David, and Dotty. They were talking in hushed tones; I assume to try to not wake me. They were all drinking coffee and Mom and Shirley were smoking. I waited a few minutes, trying to assess the situation before I wandered into the kitchen.

When I got there, Dad was peering into the living room as the other four continued talking. He had put some clothing on by then. Everyone looked exhausted and I can still remember their faces and how exhausted they all appeared. This was the one time everyone thought we would lose Sonny.

I sleepily wandered over to Mom and she hugged me while she and Shirley glanced at each other. They both knew I had no clue what was going on. Dad looked at me like he was going to say "Go back to your room" but he refrained.

Dotty poured me some orange juice and I sat on Mom's lap as she told me what had happened.

"Kev, Sonny got hurt, but he's going to be just fine. I don't want you to worry."

"But Mom, I saw blood. I'm scared," I said.

"Don't worry. Dr. Hertzberg is here, and he's patched him up and made Sonny as good as new. After the doctor leaves, Sonny is going to be sleepy for a little while so he's going to sleep on the couch before he goes home. It's very important he rests, so no bugging him, Kev, no peeping in on him. I know he's your friend, but I mean it. You leave him alone young man. Understand?"

I've never had a problem with "understanding" even back then when I was just six.

I just sometimes choose not to.

However, I was satisfied with this explanation. I went into my parents' bedroom to watch cartoons. I heard my father tell David to make sure a couple of guys were around to help Sonny get home when he woke up. He also told my mom to make sure she kept Dr. Hertzberg at our place so he could ride in the car with them and make sure Sonny got home safely. Everyone hung out in the kitchen until Sonny could be moved.

At one point, I got up during commercials to peek into the living room. I saw Sonny literally hanging over on the couch, sleeping. He had bandages on his stomach and seeing him lying there helpless made me feel incredibly sad and afraid. But there was nothing me or anyone else could do. We just had to wait and see how, and if, Sonny recovered.

It took a week or so for things to chill out.

During that time, Sonny recovered at his house which was protected around the clock by my father's guys while I saw my dad's lawyer at our house more often than I ever had before.

Geno was very worried the police would peg Sonny as the ringleader of that heist and if they did, it would get traced right back to him. He also believed if the cops couldn't find Sonny, they couldn't ask him questions, so as soon as he was well enough to travel, my dad sent him and his family up to Brattleboro, Vermont for six months where he was treated very well and had his own doctor. He and his family stayed with him until he made a full recovery. We all missed Sonny. My parents, the guys and me felt the void he left. He just had that way about him and all of us loved him. But we knew he would be back as soon as he healed, and everything had blown over. And he did come back, stronger than ever for several more years. He and my dad's organization were never fingered for that heist.

8. HOLIDAY IN THE SILVER STATE

Despite Sonny's injury, the push for cash had to continue. My dad had the Rizzo brothers take turns doing Sonny's shifts guarding the luncheonette and Little Casino. I knew he didn't feel entirely comfortable with them doing security because they were unpredictable hot heads. The brothers were loners and didn't really talk to anyone in their own time. When they were working for my dad. They understood the chain of command and always did what they were told.

To their credit, the Rizzos stepped up to the plate in a way that exceeded all expectations and really helped my dad keep the money rolling in. They were younger than most of the other members of the gang and had tons of friends in the city, which proved to be a big boon for business. Pals was doing great business during the day, and they had a crowd every night at the Little Casino. Mom told me she saw more women customers at Willie's club as well. More pretty women, (didn't matter if they were customers or employees) always meant more guys chasing them and showing off by gambling at the Little Casino and the Clubhouse so things were going great on the business end.

Mom watched the money come in and hounded my dad on a regular basis about buying a house. Geno was doing so well the occasional topic of going to Las Vegas moved from wishful thinking to a reality although Mom was not initially happy about spending house money on a trip but after my dad sold her on the idea, she started to look forward to going away on a real vacation, just her and my dad this time.

The first thing Dad did to prepare for this vacation was to trade in the dented Cadillac and buy a new one for the trip.

My dad was a Cadillac man through and through. Descriptors used in Cadillac slogans embodied everything he thought about himself: "Finest," "Magnificent," and "In a realm all its own." He saw these cars as two ton, nearly nineteen foot long, mobile, metallic manifestations of everything he considered himself to be.

This beauty was gunmetal gray with huge chrome bumpers and was considered really sharp for those days. Everyone in the gang loved and envied it. And why shouldn't they? It was the top of the line "gangster mobile." The guys admired everything my dad did and had and to keep that adoration coming in, he treated them all very well. Everyone in the Gabardine Gang drove new cars too, although none were ever as fancy as his. It wasn't unusual to see new Cadillac's and Buicks lining the street in front of Pal's, most of them gifts from my dad to his guys.

The trip to Las Vegas was planned and I was going to sit this one out. Dotty was to be my surrogate mom for two weeks and I was more than fine with that. Before they left, my mom filled the fridge at home and stocked the restaurant. She also made plans for Shirley to oversee all the family's business concerns on Barbour Street. My aunt Barbara, Mom's sister, was still living in Hartford and she was going to oversee the day-to-day household routines. We saw her regularly back then because she always needed to borrow money from my dad so keeping things running in their absence was the least, she could do as far as my parents were concerned.

Aunt Barbara preferred playing the slots to cooking and that was probably just as well. She was not a particularly good cook. She also wasn't a particularly good gambler and tended to spend her money on the "one-armed bandits," (slot machines) so my dad always had his guys keep an eye on her to make sure she stayed on a short leash.

These were not Barbara's only shortcomings my younger self was aware of. She also had four children who were all older than me. On days Dotty had class and couldn't watch after me, Barbara would bring all my punk, refrigerator-scavenging cousins with her. Every single one of them was out of control like their mother and when they were at my house, my life was a chaotic hell. I would count down the time until Dotty came home and think about my parents and the Gabardine suit heading west, riding in a brand-new Cadillac to Vegas.

Dotty was my back up mom as far as I was concerned, and she was more than capable of handling my initial distress. My mother called every chance she had and religiously sent back postcards from almost every road stop, but she did this out of love, not worry.

The trip was smooth until my parents reached the desert. At this point, the brand-new Cadillac overheated just outside of Vegas at 115 degrees, leaving them stranded on the roadside.

My dad was out of his mind with anger, my mom told Dotty when she called us at the end of the day. She told us they had been stuck for an hour or so when a state cop, of all people, stopped to help them and with his assistance, my father got the Cadillac towed to the nearest dealer.

According to my mom, Dad was like a raging bull once the car got to the repair shop. People could hear him yelling at the general manager all over the building. He was mostly right to be upset in this instance. The Cadillac only had two thousand miles on it and should never have broken down so soon although someone more reasonable might have been more rational. The intense heat had something to do with it.

Mom said she had to walk outside while my dad chewed this poor service manager up one side and down the other.

It didn't stop there; Geno got the owner of the dealership involved as well. After consulting with the owner, the manager gave my dad a new loaner Cadillac to drive while his was in the shop, and this helped calm my dad down although he was still furious. Mom told Dotty the salespeople moved all of her and Dad's belongings from their car to the loaner Cadillac to further try to appease my dad. He threw them a fifty-dollar tip and drove away.

Finally, they were back on the road and headed to their hotel. Their destination was the Golden Nugget Hotel and casino, the iconic place with the big waving cowboy sign you always see in shots of the Vegas strip on television or in the movies. My mom brought me home everything they had there with that cowboy sign on it, which was quite a collection, as you can imagine. I even got an actual cowboy outfit that looked exactly like what that big cowboy was wearing.

But my parents weren't staying there because they liked cowboys. They were there to spend some money gambling in the hotel's big casino and catch some shows.

A couple of days later, the dealer called to tell them the Cadillac was fixed and ready to pick up. My dad was more than ready. He wanted *his* car, not some loaner.

As Mom told me later, they decided to make an afternoon of it. They were going to go to lunch outside the city before they picked up the Cadillac and then she was going to hit the slot machines when they got back.

That was the plan, but it didn't work out that way.

When they got to the dealer, Dad's Cadillac was all washed, waxed and parked right at the front door. One of the salesmen walked my parents to the office where they waited for the manager. Sheepishly, as my mom put it, the manager came into the office and talked to her, not my father. He handed her the bill, which said they had replaced the thermostat and a couple of hoses and the cost of this was two hundred dollars and change. She gave it to my Dad who looked at her, turned to the manager and said, "Are you some kind of nut? You don't have the balls to give this bullshit bill to me? You give it to my wife!?!?! This car is a brand-new Cadillac, not a Goddamn Chevy!"

The manager was stumped for words, Mom said. He told my father this dealership's policy was to not provide warranty service for any car they didn't sell. Mom said she covered her eyes; she knew this was going to be another episode but added that when she peeked, she had never seen my father move so fast.

He sprang from his chair and grabbed the manager by the neck. Dad lifted this guy out of the chair with one hand and carried him up against a wall, his legs flailing. My mother said she yelled at my dad to stop, but by the time salesmen rushed into the office, my dad had gone to his dark place again and there was fire in his eyes. He kept shouting at the manager, "You WILL take care of this!"

It took no time for the entire building, including the owner, to gather in the manager's office where they saw him nod "yes" to my father who let him drop to the floor. The owner in the manager's office took the bill off the desk and ripped it up. My dad grabbed his fedora off the chair and walked through the crowd with my mom jogging behind him. They jumped in the Cadillac and drove off the lot.

I tell that story to people every now and then when they tell me that they are going to look at new cars or going to the car dealer to shop. I hope it emboldens them to be a little more aggressive with them.

My dad was not about to be hustled just because he had a Connecticut license plate, and this had both everything and nothing to do with him being a gangster.

There is no doubt Geno simply was not destined to be a steady, regular job kind of a guy.

Being a gangster is all that my father knew. Starting from an early age it was simply the only thing he knew how to do. My father wanted to make money; he just didn't want to work for it. He knew the risks and he did everything he could to minimize them, and he wasn't greedy. Like so many of the Mafia bosses you've heard about over the years, from his idol, Lucky Luciano to today's Whitey Bulger, he always took care of his family, business associates and neighbors. Sure, he profited from pretty much every transaction he made but in a strange way, it was fair. If he had had a motto, it would have been, "There's nothing wrong with a little something for 'The House.'"

While he and his organization got a cut out of every transaction, large or small in their sizable range of influence, Dad was particularly good about selling things at a fair price and he would get furious when someone he knew got ripped off or taken advantage of in any way.

Sometimes I think maybe his way should still be the way to deal with people who try to take advantage of others. It worked great back then, but today we live in a pampered society and if you do anything like my dad did that day in the dealership, you'd just end up in jail and being sued. That was life in the 50s and 60s.

My mom took the scene there in stride. This sort of thing happened at least once a week if you were around my father. And her presence kept him relatively calm. I hate to think what happened at times like this when she wasn't with him, but his crew was. While I never heard any stories about my dad "capping" someone, I'm quite certain a few people lost life and limb because they crossed him.

Things being settled at the dealership to my father's satisfaction, the vacation continued. Dad was happy to have his Cadillac back and Mom was having a blast at the slots.

They took in a bunch of shows and Hartford natives like Totie Fields and Gene Pitney headlined some of them. Totie Fields was a plus-sized comedienne who was famous for the line, "I've been on a diet for two weeks and all I've lost is fourteen days." She was also a friend of my dad's.

I remember them telling me that they would meet up for dinner with my parents a couple of nights a month.

As for Gene Pitney, you may never have heard of him, but trust me, he was a huge star then. Anyone who saw him perform in person felt incredibly lucky indeed and if you had front row seats like my mom and dad, you were exceptionally lucky. Mr. Pitney would often stop by Pal's and the Little Casino when he was back home in Hartford and my dad always treated him very well, so he was just returning the favor when my parents wanted to see his show in Vegas.

But no doubt the highlight of their trip was meeting Dean Martin. Mom had ended up sitting next to him at a casino table. I'm sure she had caught his eye, despite his girlfriend being with him. He and my dad, both being Italian, hit it off quickly and when telling the story, Dad never failed to mention Dean Martin had complimented him on his suit. The four of them grabbed a table, sat, and had drinks for a couple of hours like they were old friends.

Italians can do that.

9. A TIME OF WONDER

The trip to Vegas was just a brief respite from the Big Push for my parents. Our Big Push wasn't dissimilar to the infamous Big Dig in Boston. Seems sensible and straight forward on paper but beneath it are thousands of complexities, both known and unknown. Metaphors aside, our move was far more complicated than most people's.

Not only did we have to find a new house, my mother was now pregnant, but she still insisted on making sure everyone else living in our building had a safe, comfortable place to go.

For his part, my dad had to help with all of that and figure out how to move at least the Game Room part of his operation, which was one of his big money makers and how to keep his other businesses thriving without him being nearby all the time. This meant finding another place for the Game Room and as fate would have it, soon selling Pal's was on to his "must be done" list as well.

Any one of those things would be a project in and of itself. One person trying to do everything at once was a huge task for my father who was by no means a naturally, helpful, unselfish person but I was blissfully unaware of it at the time.

Eventually my parents narrowed their search down to two houses, one in South Windsor and one in Windsor Locks, both only about ten miles from Hartford. They ended up buying a home on a corner lot in the small town of Windsor Locks, Connecticut. My uncle Arturo had been living there for years and always wanted my dad to live closer to him and helped him find our new house. It was only a three-minute drive away from him, and Detective John had been a long-time resident in that area as well, so everyone was happy. Step one was done.

The exodus from the North End was a bitter one for the people we loved, especially Shirley and Dotty who were still living in our building. Mom felt guilty she had overlooked the fact our moving out of the city would also affect them. Everyone had to change their lifestyles, habits, even jobs. I remember Dotty and my mom cried when Mom told her we had finally bought a house and were moving.

My dad helped both of them as much as he could. He was more than generous in helping Dotty, Shirley and his working girls and members of his gang who wanted to move on when he moved.

Shirley decided to move back to Florida, but Dotty was in a different boat. She was in her final year of nursing school and had almost no money to work with. My dad felt obligated to take extra good care of her and I'd like to think knowing how much I loved her had something to do with it.

At this point, she had met a nice guy, Bob, and her life was set for certain success once she finished school. In her own stubborn way, Mom had mentally prepared herself to convince Dotty to move to the suburbs with us while she finished nursing school. But Dotty was very independent and hated the idea, even though my mother was ready to offer her whatever she wanted to keep her with us.

This impasse resulted in the three of them having some serious late-night conversations and some talks just between my parents. My mom was not about to let Dotty try to live on her own without help and it seemed unlikely Dotty could be persuaded into moving to Windsor Locks. After several nights of these discussions, my parents came up with a plan.

My dad came up with two plans which would smooth this transition for both women.

My dad insisted Dotty stay with us one way or the other until we moved, and he found her a safe apartment close to school. Even though she could have stayed in the building, there was no way he was going to leave her there virtually alone and unprotected amidst the growing neighborhood tension, even with his guys around. It took some convincing, but Dotty finally agreed this was sensible. Plus, she could still help my mom by continuing to watch me while we packed and moved. This was the plan that made my mom happy.

Privately, he told my mom that maybe once Dotty saw how nice the new house was and the reality of seeing us pack sunk in, she would change her mind and decide to come with us. But he also knew this was unlikely, so he was also making plans to set Dotty up in her own place.

My dad sent his guys out to talk to various landlords who owned Victorian houses in a neighborhood close to the hospital where the school was. Many of these turns of the century houses had been converted into apartment buildings. The gabardine gang's mission was to get her into her own apartment in one of the row houses next to Hartford Hospital, the plan was to get her near the nursing school she attended. A nice place on the same street.

Each day, my dad spent an hour or two on the phone with his guys talking about what they found. No matter how much my mom wanted her with us, Dad knew he would be able to get Dotty set up in no time, but he could also make it take long enough to make the transition a little smoother for everyone. Having connections, power and money can make things happen quick or slow, whichever is more convenient.

Shortly before our moving date, Henry and Johnny K toured a place and it was perfect. A huge, clean three-bedroom apartment in an Old Victorian house in a safe, quiet neighborhood within walking distance to the school and a market. They reported back to my dad about it but told him there was a problem. After talking to the landlord, Mr.

Kellerman, for a couple of hours, they could come nowhere close on negotiating the rent.

Mr. Kellerman wanted around three hundred dollars a month, which at that time was considered rent only a doctor could afford. In fact, a visiting resident doctor was the tenant vacating the space.

My dad knew this Kellerman guy. He was a rich Jewish investor who also owned a few buildings on Barbour Street and was an occasional patron of the Little Casino. Mr. Kellerman, as my dad described him, he was "a stubborn and cheap son-of-a-bitch who gives nothing away."

He also had never done business with my dad.

When Dotty came by to see us that night, as she did every night when she got out of school, Dad didn't let on about the apartment.

My mom didn't even know about it.

My mom was going to try and convince Dotty one last time to move to the suburbs with us. However, my dad had quite different plans. Mom had the closing date for the house circled on the calendar with a big red circle; it was coming up quick.

But before Dotty came over, I heard dad tell Henry to meet him at the Victorian house the next day with Johnny. I knew if my dad wanted a meeting, it was something serious. My dad had put his plan into motion and never let my mom know what he was doing. That happened more than usual.

The next morning rolled around and when I got up, our Cadillac wasn't in the driveway. No one thought much of it, and we all went about our business.

That night, my dad came home with huge sausage grinders from an Italian place on the other side of town. When he came home with sausage grinders, it was a sure sign he was in a good mood. He couldn't wait to talk to Dotty and told Mom to go downstairs and leave a note on her door to come and see us as soon as she got in. Little notes were the low-tech way you contacted people before email although this was unnecessary.

Dotty would come up to our apartment every night. We were always her first stop. A couple of hours later, Mom saw Dotty drive in, and she came up to join us.

We sat around the table talking and eating when my dad suddenly turned to Dotty and shouted, "Start packing your things." Dotty had a puzzled look on her face.

Conversation stopped and the two women were confused, especially my mom. In her mind, Dotty was moving in with us and the date was still a few weeks away. Dad sprang his news as he always did, loud and to the point.

"You have a three-bedroom apartment in a Victorian mansion just two blocks from the hospital. You can move in whenever you want, and the rent is paid for a year!" my dad began to laugh.

My mom was totally confused. Yet, she was excited that Dotty got what she wanted. Dotty and my mom burst into tears of joy.

Once the tears stopped, my mom did a Jekyll and Hyde. She snapped her head around and gave my dad a dead eye stare. "Why the hell didn't you tell me you were doing this, I had everything planned!" she yelled at him, genuinely mad. My dad just laughed hard at her reaction and Dotty started to laugh at her too.

Dad said, in a rare moment of true kindness, "You know she wants to be on her own. She'll be perfectly fine there."

Mom reconciled herself with this once she understood more about the place and learned Bob, Dotty's boyfriend, would be able to stay with her. She was totally okay with "Plan B" after a few minutes. Dotty hugged my parents then ran downstairs to call Bob.

Everything had worked out in the end with a little help from my dad.

I already knew my dad considered Mr. Kellerman cheap and stubborn, but his personal visit to him earlier that day, along with Henry and Johnny K for backup, changed those qualities about Mr. Kellerman, at least temporarily.

As the story goes, my dad began the conversation by telling Mr. Kellerman exactly what he thought of him. It was a lengthy list with nothing good on it. Mr. Kellerman was offended by this and quickly attempted to muster a defense, but my dad backed down to no one and quickly lost what little patience he had.

He walked out to his Cadillac, with Johnny and Henry standing watching him with one eye and Mr. Kellerman with the other, in disbelief. Given his rage, they feared my dad was going to get his "big boy" (what he and his gang referred to as his shot gun) to beat the shit (or worse) out of Mr. Kellerman.

Instead, he opened the trunk and grabbed a brand new, full-length mink coat, with labels and the chain still attached to it.

He brought it into the house. He threw the coat on the table and asked Mr. Kellerman, "Your wife likes mink?"

Mr. Kellerman flashed a sheepish grin, nodded, and responded, "My wife loves mink."

"This fucking coat will cover the rent there for one year. Give Dotty the God damn apartment for that year, or my second offer won't be so nice."

They shook hands.

Deal done.

My dad always kept some score items for times like those. Apparently, this coat was part of an old haul from a couple of years before. Dotty got her apartment and money hungry Mr. Kellerman got a five-thousand-dollar mink coat for three thousand dollars in rent.

When I got older, I wondered what would have happened if Mr. Kellerman had said "no."

I knew why Johnny "Knucks," the former prizefighter, had been there. His mere presence was to help Mr. Kellerman make the right decision.

What I didn't learn until later was that Dad also had the building inspector in his pocket. If Johnny's presence weren't enough, he would have simply had the building condemned.

My dad had that kind of power, so Mr. Kellerman was wise to recognize it and give in.

The pretty ladies on the second floor (there was always a constant change over with them) stayed on Barbour Street for a year or so, giving them time to relocate. Then the owner sold the building and paid back my father the rest of what he owed.

Right before we moved, my mom gave birth to my brother, Ralph.

Ralph was a sickly baby. He had ear infections and was constantly being rushed to the hospital with high fevers. One infection was so bad it nearly killed him and by being so sick and frail early on is a large part of the reason he became my parent's favorite child.

A year or two after we moved, Sonny moved away from the Barbour Street neighborhood as well. The injury from his shooting became too much of a problem as he got older and from then on, we only saw him once a year or so.

He ended up becoming a union rep in the construction trade for many years.

Dad was okay with Sonny doing his thing. Unlike the real high-end mobsters, these lower echelon guys were free to leave the group to pursue other ventures. They were more like freelance criminals who swore their allegiance to one group at a time. My dad left managing the big-ticket boosting items to the guys back in the city. They were still part of the gang who just did what they always did. They just did it without my dad around to supervise.

As for Jinx, while it broke our hearts, we gave him to Sam the Butcher. Jinx was a German Shepherd security dog who had been trained to hate Black people and had developed a taste for blood. The people that trained Jinx sold the German Shepards to neighborhoods that were rough and unsafe. They were trained with the German language. With many of the thugs moving onto the street. They were new to how the system worked. The gang used to say that if they were stupid enough to break into a gangster building, a dog was the least of their worries. Although it didn't happen often Jinx chased more than a few thieves down the street screaming. My mom thought it best to not bring him into a new neighborhood full of people he didn't know. After all he was trained to stop people and especially people of color that were trying to steal from others.

Sam was the perfect new owner for Jinx. He loved dogs and would take him to his shop for security. Being a butcher, he always had great leftovers, so Jinx was always well fed. Other than putting on a couple of pounds, Jinx and Sam were happy to carry on, living life the way they wanted. I missed Jinx, but I knew that his calling was to protect and that's what he loved to do.

Our new house at 22 Laurel Road was a small three-bedroom ranch, the color of day-old bologna. My mother loved the huge kitchen with the pink General Electric stove and matching oven. There were windows above the sink that looked out on the backyard. The living room had a small fireplace which came in handy on winter days when we lost power, which was not uncommon during frequent New England blizzards.

The bedrooms were down the hallway where the bathroom was and were arranged in a "T" shape. All the rooms were much larger than the ones on Barbour Street and I was thrilled to have more room to display my growing collection of Roy Rogers's paraphernalia and my newfound love of everything related to football.

Once we got settled in, my dad converted the two-car garage into what we called "The Playroom." It had a large, black, heavy padded leather bar and matching high back chairs.

If these furnishings sound familiar, that's because they were. It was the same bar set up that had been in The Little Casino. The Playroom also had a slot machine, air conditioning for the summer, a Ben Franklin fireplace for the winter, nice carpets and of course, a couple of televisions and a phone. It was more of my dad's "Man Cave" than anything although it was the party room for holidays and special occasions.

I could tell that my mom was relieved to be out of the suburban life and have a real house. City living was not high on my mother's list of favorite things, but she missed Dotty a lot and I did, too.

There are some moments in one's life that seem to be burned into your memory and our first night in the new house is one of those moments for me. I remember it because once we got there, my dad suddenly insisted, much to my mother's chagrin, that all the carpets be pulled up and taken out. "I'm not going to live in other people's filth," he screamed. Hence, our first nights in our new house were with cold tiled floors and minimal furniture.

My uncle Arturo (Art) his wife, Lil, and their three children, Leslie, Janet and Arturo Junior, or "Johnny" as we called him, all a little older than me, had helped us move some things and for dinner, we ordered big sausage grinders and pizza from a local shop. Everyone gathered and ate in the big living room that echoed since it now lacked rugs and the drapes hadn't been put up yet. We sat huddled in front of yet another mammoth, brand new, state of the art black and white television set, glued to a new episode of "The Twilight Zone."

We spent the summer settling into our new house. It was strange not to hear car horns honking, music and people yelling across the buildings. In fact, we heard nothing. It was a quiet suburb.

Mom loved her house and our neighborhood. It was free from all the racial tension that had been building up on

Barbour Street. While our neighbors were predominately white, we had a handful of neighbors from other races and nationalities, and everyone got along great. This was just what she had longed for.

Mom was beyond excited about the fresh start, the fact that the elementary school was only three streets away and that she could grow her own garden and I was excited too. We had a big yard to play football and baseball. The day came when Mom took me to the local school to enroll me for first grade and I finally had that to look forward to. I hadn't spent much time with children my own age and I wanted very much to make some friends in my new town.

My dad was making the daily ten-mile trip to Pal's. I know my dad didn't like making that drive but it was a necessity. He still had to finish moving the Little Casino and the Game Room closer to Windsor Locks and he had found a place to relocate those operations.

My dad reluctantly moved his little operation to the next town over from ours. He moved the Little Casino and the entire operation of the Game Room to a new private building in Windsor, Connecticut, about ten minutes from our new house on Laurel Road.

The "Clubhouse," as my dad and his friends called it, was tucked behind a factory in the industrial part of town. Henry knew someone who owned that property for a tax write off and he was able to cut a deal with them so my dad could use it to set up shop.

At one time, The Clubhouse must have been the home of the factory owner, although it was more like a fortress than a house, which is why I always thought my dad liked it. The front yard faced the back of the factory and there was a huge parking lot between the two properties. Chain link fences surrounded the Clubhouse and the parking lot and divided them. The back of the Clubhouse overlooked the end of a small, dead end, tree lined suburban street which was dotted with small houses similar to ours.

The location of the Clubhouse was perfect for what my dad and his guys wanted to do. It was also much larger than its previous location and it quickly filled up with all the gear necessary to run the operation.

The Clubhouse business was a very low-key operation, except for Sundays when the neighbors probably noticed an influx of Cadillacs driven around by cigar smoking, fedora wearing men who would go in and out of there all day.

This was okay with the neighbors. They were all Italian and either knew my dad and the Gabardine Gang already or knew about them.

Dad's first order of business was moving and setting up the Game Room in the Clubhouse which became like a living creature.

Like any other living creature, The Clubhouse had a heart and a pulse, both of which smelled like smoke and booze.

Its heart was the living room which was full of scatter rugs and comfortable second-hand couches with hard wooden arms and matching chairs where the guys did their work. Things were always spilled there so the new furniture was pointless. Conveniently located near all the furniture and televisions was a big metal cooler with sliding doors that had once been in Pal's. That's where all the beer and wine, as well as a couple of six packs of soda were kept, hence all the spills. One wall was lined with television sets, each with a different game on. There were only three networks then, not like today when you can watch multiple games from multiple channels on one giant HDTV.

On the opposite wall were a couple of big ass grey metal desks where the guys did paperwork. Each desk had several transistors and short-wave radios on it and the guys would use them to keep track of games and other sporting events they couldn't get on TV. If they couldn't get something on the radio, they would use the short-wave radios to contact people from states where games they were interested in were being played so they could get the scores. They booked all sports, but since football was my dad's favorite, it was mine, too and for many years, even on days we weren't getting along, we always watched the Sunday games together.

There were several phones in the living room as well. The guys had associates at tracks up and down the East Coast; New York tracks like Belmont and Saratoga being the staples. Gamblers would call the Clubhouse and in turn, the Clubhouse would call the tracks my dad's guys manned, and bets were placed that way.

The pulse of the operation was in the repurposed master bedroom. This room had several of the same metal desks and office chairs in the living room and about a dozen phones with a bunch of guys and girls answering them. Their job was to take people's bets. They would take the gambler's name, bet and the team or event and write it down on a note pad using a system much like the one used at Pal's for loans. It was the hottest Bookie room in the area. Taking bets on just about every sport from football, horse racing, boxing, car racing etc. They used two methods of saving notes, one was in code and the other was with dissolving paper. The phone calls coming into that room took precedence over everything, which is why the guys in the living room used the short-wave radio to get their information whenever possible.

In a sense, the Gabardine Gang was 'way ahead of their time. They were essentially running an off-track betting operation before it was invented. It was really a high-tech system in a day when there was no tech at all.

At the end of the day, all the bets would be tallied, and hand entered one book and one exact duplicate copy of them in another book. Once that was done, all the notes for the day were destroyed. Except for the notes given to the collection guys that were written with dissolvable ink so in case they were questioned by anyone, everything would disappear with just a couple of drops of water.

They used decoys for their accounting books.

Someone would take a regular reading book, strip off its cover and spine, and glue them onto a blank ledger book where all the bets and customers were recorded.

Shakespeare, Poe, Mary Shelley, *Gone with the Wind*. They had all the classics! I was about six or seven years old when I quickly learned these books weren't books for reading, I found that out when I found a copy of *Moby Dick* on a desk one day and picked it up to read. I was surprised to see it was just pages of names and numbers in different sequences. I put it back on the desk and never said a word to my dad about it. I would have gotten the belt for that for sure!

My dad kept one copy of each book under a false floor in the Clubhouse attic and Henry would take the other one home with him. They kept the books for a week or two until all the debts were collected, and then those books were burned.

Old School redundancy and back up at its best!

Uncollected bets were another story, but I never heard about them "whacking" anyone for money. What I do know is if someone had assets and owed them, anything they had would be seized until the payment was squared. Cars, jewelry, houses, even horses. That was how the gang got their money back from people who couldn't pay it up.

It took me a while to learn the term "The Clubhouse" also could refer to a building at the golf course.

I would hear guys I had never seen around my dad's place talk about "The Clubhouse" and wonder how they knew about my dad's secret place, although of course, I never asked them about it. Later I learned they were simply talking about the golf course, which was never of any interest to my dad or his crew.

While my dad's clubhouse was no doubt a business, it wasn't all work.

The kitchen had a bunch of small, commercial equipment from Pal's, a big industrial slicer, dozens of chef's knives, huge pots and pans. The basement housed a monster refrigerator which was always loaded with deli meats and there was a big freezer down there as well.

On days when things were in full swing, there were a couple of "waitresses" there who would make sandwiches for everyone working the phones. They'd also come in a couple of times during the week to clean up and get things ready for the next business day.

The one constant woman there was Marny. Marny had long thick red hair, even longer legs, and an hourglass figure. She had been an exotic dancer Dad and the guys had met on one of their many trips to Florida. She had fallen for one of the goons and they became a couple. She moved up to Connecticut with him because she wanted to be part of the excitement.

Things worked out well for Marny up there. The guys tipped her well and she made boatloads of money, much more than she ever did as a dancer. Plus, she always wanted kids, so I became like a kid to her when I was there, and she became almost like a Dotty to me. Whenever I showed up, she would drop whatever she was doing and get me ice cream or food.

It wasn't long before the neighborhood in Windsor was in many ways, very similar to Barbour Street. Local police patrolled the area and became some of my dad's best customers. No one complained. In fact, the neighbors were thrilled their road was now more secure than Fort Knox. And my mom was thrilled she was no longer under the same roof of my dad's business and was, in fact, in a totally different town.

Even though I was only occasionally allowed to go to the Clubhouse and hang out with the guys, I always had fun there. And back in those days, my father always spent time with me. On Saturdays he'd take me back to our old neighborhood. We'd go to Pal's and always tried to squeeze in on a visit with Dotty.

It was around then I started putting the pieces regarding my father's business and friends together. A lot of what I know about those days come from the answers I got to asking a ton of questions, especially when I hit school age! (I'm still like that. When I need information, I'll ask endless questions until I get it.)

There were times when with my dad that I thought he liked having a son to do things with. I remember the time we piled in the car: me, Dad, Uncle Art, and my cousins, to go to Fenway Park and see a Red Sox game. It's been a few years but there is nothing quite as exciting as walking up the ramp and seeing the field at Fenway Park. Everything is in Technicolor it seems. It really is breath taking.

It was the mid-1960s and our "big city" Cadillac had been joined by a nice suburban top of the line station wagon with wood paneled sides.

We drove straight to Fenway Park and seeing the light stands from outside the stadium always excited me.

My dad circled around the blocks near the stadium, looking for the cheapest place to park. He picked a gas station just outside the park. He and my uncle knew that "sardine parking" was a norm on game day but my dad already knew he planned on leaving before the rush and as we pulled in, he told the operator to give him a spot where he could get out early. The game was horrible, and the Sox got shelled. My cousins and I ate and had fun, until my dad wanted to leave in the seventh inning. Uncle Art was quick tempered like my dad, and he wanted to stay but he just gave in this time. Since the game was a bust, he agreed with my dad we should hit the road and miss all the traffic getting back to Connecticut.

We got out of the stadium and walked over to the garage only to see Dad's station wagon "sardined" into a spot that would take moving no less than six cars to get out.

Geno was livid!

He went to the booth and told the guy there he had paid extra so we could leave early and not have this parking situation happen to us. Unfortunately, this wasn't the same guy he had dealt with earlier. We could hear him screaming from the street where we were standing.

"Listen you mongrel! You call your boss right now and get my fucking car out of that mess."

The guy looked at my dad and casually said, "Nothing I can do," which wasn't the right thing to say to anyone, let alone my father.

I saw my dad grab this clueless attendant and literally drag him out of the booth. Uncle Art ran over to stop my father, but it was too late. My dad had already thrown the attendant on top of the car in front of ours and slapped him four or five times in the face as the guy fell to the ground.

"You dirty son of a bitch! You rotten fucking drunk! You have five minutes to get my car the hell of that Goddamn mess!" my dad screamed.

He then grabbed the guy off the ground and dragged him back to the booth and made him call the owner.

The attendant handed my dad the phone but smoothing things over with the owner wasn't possible only seconds into the conversation.

Geno said, "Who's this?" and the owner replied with a Jewish last name and my father went off on him as well. Like I said, he hated anyone who wasn't Italian. However, my dad did like the Jewish people. Just not so much on this day!

"Listen to me, you Jew bastard. I'm going to knock all the teeth out of this mongrel's head if you don't get your kike ass down here right now and get my car out, you stoogatz (dick)!"

My dad grabbed the attendant by the neck again and shoved the phone back in his ear.

"Get his car out!" the attendant yelled to the owner of the station as my father yanked the phone back from him still holding him by the collar, dropping the phone.

"You stupid son of a bitches, I told you that I wanted to get out early, I outta break your fucking skull for this," as the attendant trembled. It couldn't have been more than five minutes when the owner drove in with all the car keys. Not sure if my dad was still mad, he apologized, and he and the attendant moved all the cars out of the way so my dad could get out. My dad then said to the owner, "You Putz, give me my money back too and fung gool (fuck you) & fanabila (go to Hell)

The owner gave Dad his money and off we went.

Things in the suburbs settled into routine after a while and it was quite peaceful. I liked going to school and Mom kept busy running the household, taking care of Ralph, and keeping the Clubhouse stocked.

That November my dad loaded me into our Cadilliac, and we took a trip over to the Clubhouse. When we got there, the whole gang was waiting, including Marny. Even some of the guys who only occasionally worked for my dad and a couple of the part time waitresses were there! Everyone was in a great mood; smoking, drinking, and eating, but no one was working so I knew something fun was up.

A big box truck pulled up in front of the Clubhouse early that cold afternoon. Everyone put on their coats and hats to go out and help unload the cargo. I went out too, because of course, I was dying to see for myself what was in that truck. Some of the guys opened the back and all I could see was stacks of boxes, all uniform in size—boxes and boxes of partially frozen turkeys.

Some of the crew had hijacked a big truck full of turkeys, cleared it out and stored them in a giant commercial freezer until my dad could move them.

That year my dad had devised a plan to give everyone in both our old neighborhood and our two new ones (the

Clubhouse area included), a Thanksgiving turkey. No matter what color or religion you were, if you were having a tough time financially that year, my dad was going to see to it you and your family had a turkey.

All the guys pulled up their Cadillac, popped open the trunks, loaded them up with boxes of turkeys and scattered in all directions.

My dad was in a great mood, despite this being a rare occasion when he wasn't making money from something. He and the rest of the Gabardine Gang truly got a kick out of being Robin Hood and his Merry Men that day.

The guys delivered turkeys right to everyone's front door, both on Barbour Street and Laurel Street in Windsor Locks and the dead-end street behind the Clubhouse. My dad even brought home enough turkeys for all our relatives.

My grandfather, Raphelle DiBacco, originating from Italy, captured in the early 1900s.

Young Geno DiBacco and family friend
hanging out in Hartford in the 1930s.

Geno, the wannabe gangster, circa the mid-1930s.

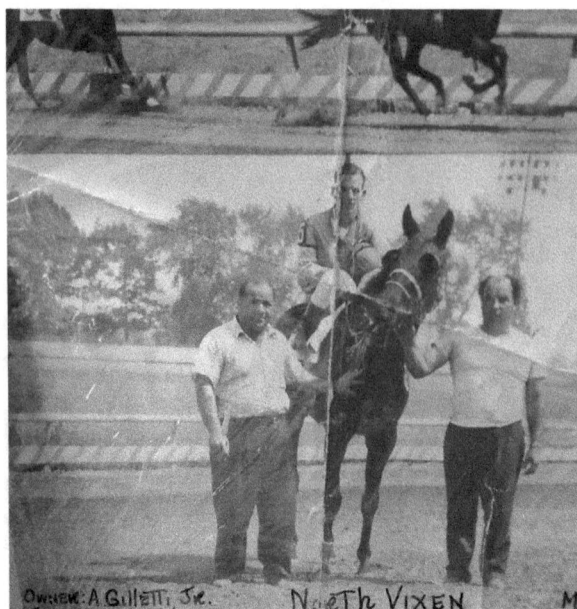

Geno DiBacco, with his partner Anthony, proudly presented their first racehorse in the 1950s.

Geno DiBacco's trip to Las Vegas with Rena in the 1950s.

Rena and Geno DiBacco at a Las Vegas Casino, 1950s.

Sam 'The Butcher' alongside Geno DiBacco at the dog track, featuring Geno's Greyhound in the 1950s.

One of Geno's guys, in the 1950s.

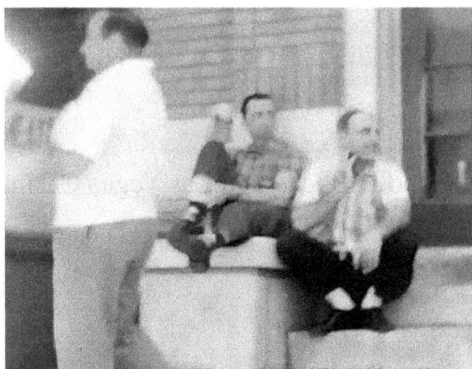

A trio of gang members casually gathered
outside Pal's Luncheonette in the 1950s.

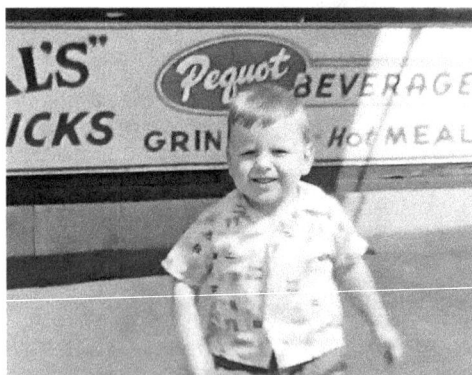

Kevin DiBacco in front of Pal's Luncheonette, 1960s.

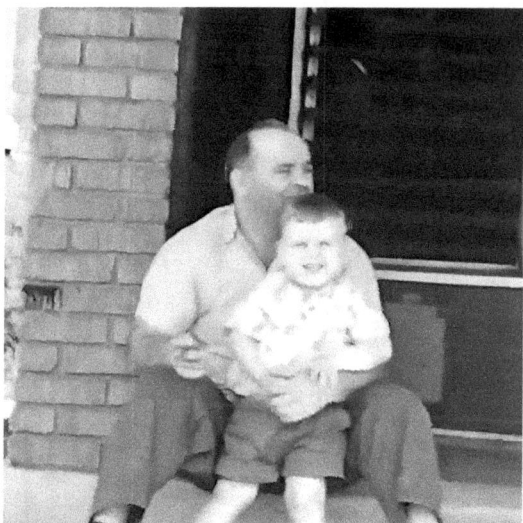

Kevin and Geno DiBacco are on Pal's stoop, while
Rena captures the moment on film, the 1960s.

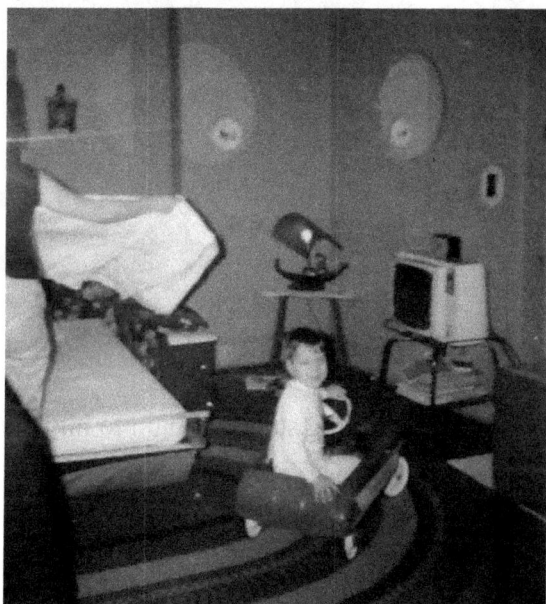

Kevin riding around living room of
Barbour St. apartment in the 1960s.

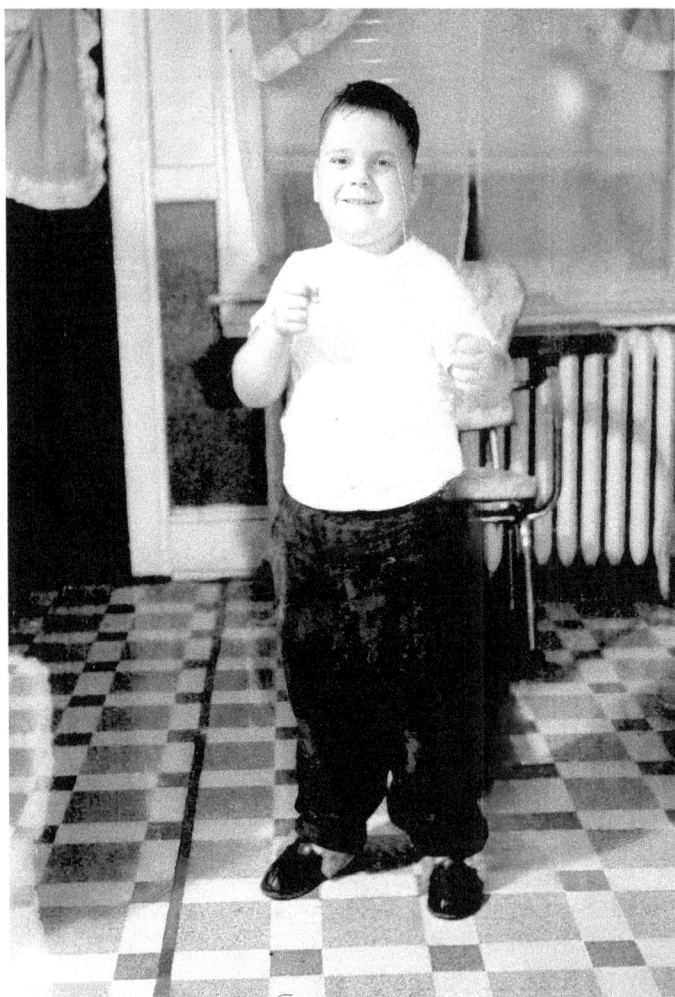

Kevin posing in boxing stance, taught to him 1960s.

10. 1968 - THE PREACHER AND THE MOBSTER

The tepid racial change which had slowly been happening in Hartford reached a rapid boil almost overnight after the United States Congress passed the Civil Rights Act in July 1964, ending legal segregation. My mom wasn't pleased her prediction had come true, but she sure was happy we were out of there and safe.

It took only three years after we left Barbour Street for things to change quickly and dramatically. Our old neighborhood went from seventy percent white to seventy percent, or more, Black in just those few years.

Unlike the South back then, there was no official segregation in Hartford. In fact, during the Civil War, Hartford was one of the seats of the Abolitionist movement. But "official" is the operative word in describing Hartford's opinion of segregation. Like many New Englanders, Hartfordians were pleased Black people were no longer slaves, but that was the extent of their charity. Most people agreed that they deserve a shot just like anybody else. But you are not given a handout, you work for it.

Black people moving into their old, all white neighborhoods was a different matter entirely.

But nothing could be done to stop it, no matter what anyone did or said. Things were headed for a permanent change.

The Barbour Street neighborhood had been sleepy, safe, and productive when my dad and his guys patrolled the streets. Now, there were new Black run groups in that area, some organized, some not and one thing they had in common was they all used the North End as a rallying point. The NAACP, CORE, SNCC and even the Black Panthers gained a foothold there with a united message. They demanded better housing, cleaner streets and parks, more traffic lights, and a better response time from local police. These groups were the good guys, but they were far outnumbered by thugs who just wanted to cause trouble. With the local self-policing from the Gabardine Gang all but gone, they did exactly that.

The Barbour Street neighborhood became a crime zone with burnt-out buildings, abandoned cars, streetwalkers, and drug dealers. Local supermarkets were constantly robbed as were the liquor stores, drug stores and even the mini marts. It didn't matter what color the business owners were, the troublemakers were intent on destruction.

Residents who stayed there after we left were disgusted by the lack of self-respect and self-control the new influx of disrespectful residents brought with them. Many of the hard-working Black people who were among the first to move into the neighborhood looking for a better life were afraid as well. As a result of this turn for the worst, many of the old Italian and Jewish families who had made this place their home for generations did what we did and moved to the suburbs.

During this tumultuous time, there were many nights when the Black business owners who my dad had helped over the years returned the favor and stood guard in front of Pal's when he and the gang weren't around. They kept looters and thugs off the property. Many of these men cared a lot about my dad and appreciated all he had done to keep the neighborhood a safe place. But even as all the local business owners rallied together to protect their livelihoods, they found this to be an increasingly impossible task.

It was at this time that my dad made the decision to sell Pal's and work exclusively from the Clubhouse.

This was when Reverend Richard Brooks, the minister of Mount Olive Baptist Church, just a few blocks away, entered our lives.

Reverend Brooks and my dad were about the same age and if you are inclined to be charitable, I guess you could say they were both activists and "take charge" kind of guys although admittedly they were on vastly different paths.

By now you know Geno was a pro-white, pro-Italian guy. Reverend Brooks was a pro-civil right, pro Black kind of a guy. Even though they were worlds apart in many ways, they had one overriding thing in common. They both wanted to do right for their people and their neighborhood.

I remember the day Reverend Brooks and his entourage stopped by Pal's for a meeting with my dad. Some of the members of the Reverend's contingent had also joined some of the Black militant groups who disliked white-owned businesses in the neighborhood. These groups had already made it clear their intention was to pipe bomb all the white businesses that didn't leave the area, and this included Pal's. Reverend Brooks and my dad both wanted a peaceful solution to that.

I watched from across the room as the well-dressed men and my dad talked.

The Reverend proposed my dad sell Pal's to his brother, Adam, so the luncheonette could stay a part of the community.

My dad saw this as another win. He had spent enough time in the suburbs to know there wasn't anything left for him in the North End. The Reverend's proposal was a perfect way for my dad to leave the area and still be able to keep the old place going for the locals.

When the meeting concluded, all the men shook hands.

Back in Windsor Locks that night, my dad told my mom what had happened and the outcome. My mom was more than pleased. In her mind, she wasn't sure how much longer my dad would have been able to keep the business open.

It was only a matter of time before things got even worse. Knowing they were targeted; the locals were looking to fight to protect the area.

The year was 1967.

My dad had escaped any kind of violence and kept the restaurant in the neighborhood.

Pal became "Brooks Luncheonette."

Unfortunately for the Reverend and his brother, the militant youth who had attended the meeting became part of a small, unorganized group of thugs. These guys had no respect for authority, the church or even themselves. The authorities and the locals began to think that militant groups like the Black Panthers were responsible for not just attacking white-owned businesses; they looted and burned down Black-owned businesses as well. The neighborhood which had thrived for decades was now just a shadow of itself.

The luncheonette and the Brooks family became targets for the very people they tried to help. What had once been Pal's had bricks thrown through the windows and was looted on almost a weekly basis.

As for the Reverend Brooks and his brother, Adam, the militants they tried to befriend and work with deemed them "Uncle Toms" and sellouts. It even got to the point where their homes were vandalized, and Reverend Brooks ended up with police patrols sitting in front of his home to protect him and his family. He had tried to preach the word of Martin Luther King and find a peaceful solution, but it did not happen that way at all.

One balmy day in July, a Black youth named William Toules verbally assaulted a waitress at Brooks. His release from jail after his bail was posted sparked three days of the most violent riots the city of Hartford had ever seen. A wild group of youths firebombed the West Bar Supermarket,

Sam's meat market, the liquor store and of course, Brooks Luncheonette, and chaos ensued.

At home, my dad was heartbroken watching TV and seeing our old neighborhood on fire.

Many of the former residents from there have never forgotten those horrific days and blame the entire problem on Reverend Brooks and other Civil Rights leaders who they believe whipped people into a frenzy. Without sitting down to talking out a solution.

But we were safe at our new Windsor Locks home although my parents wondered about what was going to happen to the friends they left behind.

11. TAXIS AND BABIES

With Pal's sold and The Clubhouse pretty much just used on the weekends and a few nights a week. My dad was in a bit of a bind in terms of cash flow. The slot machines and roulette wheel from the Little Casino were put in storage. Half a dozen or so slot machines were moved to The Clubhouse and one which ended up in our garage. The days of small stakes games at the Little Casino and the Game Room were over.

While in the back of his mind Dad always knew he would have to sell Pal's, it surprised him how quickly it had happened and that was a problem. He had counted on the income from there for at least another year or two while he and the gang changed revenue streams. In addition, having to go down there all the time to manage things gave him something to do and got him out of the house, both of which my mother supported.

Never one to ever consider traditional employment, my dad and the gang decided to concentrate on what they hoped to be more lucrative areas of organized crime: sports booking, horse and dog racing and increasing their business of acquiring and fencing high end goods.

Fencing was where the money was, and my dad came up with a way to do it that was sheer genius. If people couldn't come to him, he and his crew would go to them. It wasn't until years later I learned the scope of this venture.

They already had a highly organized system. These guys got tips from almost everyone about when trucks and trains carrying shipments of interest were coming in or passing through. If they had luxury items like cameras, gold, diamonds or jewelry, the guys would knock them off and take everything to David to be evaluated. After that, here's where Dad's genius distribution plan and his new immigrant friend, Patel, came into play.

Patel had moved to the United States from India with a boatload of cash. A few years after he arrived, he had the idea of opening a taxi business in Hartford, and that's what he did. He was a frequent visitor to the Little Casino, which is how my father learned Patel had purchased a fleet of taxi cabs. It was called "City Cab," and they ran all over the city and state.

My dad offered Patel a cut of his new high-end merchandise business venture.

In exchange, my dad would drive one of Patel's taxis part-time. My dad was not a people person, so this was an odd move to everyone. No one knew exactly what my dad was thinking.

It all went back to his heist operation. David still evaluated the products, and the merchandise was shipped to buyers around the country. But after my dad put his plan in place, everything going in and out of this operation was being transported to and from the airport, bus stations, train stations and local customers in the trunks of modified taxis.

The trunks in several of Patel's cabs had false bottoms under where the spare tires were stored. Some days, they had doctor's bags full of cash. Other days, it was boxes full of valuables, all ready to be shipped.

In fact, there was one time that the score was plutonium.

Dad asked if I wanted to see what was in the trunk that day, and of course I did. I was too young to understand what plutonium was or what it was used for. All I knew was it was the first shipment I had even seen all packaged in metal containers, neatly tucked into their spaces, not only was this highly illegal, but it was also extremely dangerous and at the height of the Cold War, possession of radioactive materials had espionage implications as well.

Remember, airport security back then was nothing like it is today. Boxes weren't even x-rayed there. Boxes of diamonds and watches, or radioactive material for that matter, just looked like a box of machine parts or sweaters and that's all anyone cared about.

On any given day, the City Cabs were hauling stolen merchandise around the city and as far as Boston and New York. No one suspected a thing; it all looked normal as the taxis flew around the city. It was a brilliant idea, and it went on uninterrupted for as long as I can remember.

I saw these hauls quite a few times because, much to my mother's chagrin, my dad began to start stopping home more and more often on his way to the airport. Our house was much closer to the airport than the Clubhouse and sometimes, against my mother's wishes, he and the guys would box the West Coast shipments there. This situation cramped my mom's style because he was always so grumpy, and things would often get a little tense when my dad came home unannounced.

My dad was angry for years after losing the luncheonette. The fact that he had to alter his lifestyle, left him in a permanent pissed off mood. My father could never be described as "sunny." Geno started to become a cranky, grumpy Old Italian. Plus, the new system wasn't generating the same amount of money as the Little Casino had.

My mom wanted to make life in the suburbs enjoyable, despite my father's scaly attitude. My mom did her best to fix up the house and make it more of a home. As time went on my dad got consistently thriftier and left her with little money to work with. The newfound cheap streak had her really concerned. Gone were the days of new furniture and wads of cash to shop with. We started getting hand-me-down furniture from friends and relatives.

It wasn't long before my mom knew she would have to go back to work to keep the house running the way she wanted. He gave her a set limit for food and other expenses and that was it.

Blowing wads of cash, gambling and taking trips was one thing to my dad. Spending money on new appliances, furniture and drapes for the house was a total waste of money in his mind. Finally, she had enough and took a full-time job in a small assembly line plant.

My father started to blame the Blacks for the loss of his big income and that's when we saw his hatred toward them really come out.

He was not alone.

Back then, Blacks and Italians never got along. His crew also despised the change in their lifestyles, the change in the neighborhood the new Black residents brought along with them.

While my dad had money and my mother's constant nagging to get him to move to the suburbs, most of his crew had no choice but to stay in the North End and fight to take back what was theirs, starting with the local economy.

You see, to them, civil rights riots like the one that started at Brooks place were just a temporary slowdown for the local businesses. These guys held such a grudge they were willing to go on a mission to choke the local economy by disrupting all commerce going into the neighborhood just to make the point they were in control.

As seasoned hijackers with informants everywhere, on the payroll, they already knew when shipments were coming in and by which routes. Their targets had always been small, high-end items but they expanded to whatever wasn't nailed down. Because of them, most of the food, alcohol, medicine, and clothing on order never made it to businesses in the North End.

Now merchants there had another problem. Not only was there chaos in their neighborhood, but shipments weren't making it there, thanks to this offshoot of the Gabardine Gang.

With my dad's okay, they set up crews in each section of the city. By this time, recruiting people to work with them was amazingly easy. It wasn't just the Italians. Many of the Irish, Asian, and other ethnic populations were not afraid to show their anger toward one ethnic race trying to forcefully remove people that have been there for generations.

In fact, Franklin Avenue, in the "Little Italy" section town became ground zero for the volatile race relations fight. The white population refused to be burned out of their city by a group of people that were not willing to buy them out. The goal of the Black Panthers and militants was to burn the business out. This was a huge problem for the business owners that worked hard. The locals set up boundaries and no Black militants were allowed to enter that area. With the neighborhood cops, they formed and organized vigilante groups to patrol the area. This kind of neighborhood self-policing continues there to this day.

Despite these rather obvious warnings, often, the militants chose to ignore them, a course of action that was not at all successful. These vigilante groups were so good on their own there was only one time Dad and his personal crew had to get involved.

"Why these niggers thought they could just walk in and change a neighborhood because they simply wanted to was beyond all logical thinking," was how my dad always framed the beginning of this story.

Like that and with a laugh.

He also told this story to anyone who would listen.

It happened on a scorching summer day in 1969, a serious and violent time in Hartford.

Word on the street was that on that day, some Black Panthers, as well as members of some other groups were going to gather. They planned to make a show of force to demonstrate that from that time forward, they were going to take over the white areas.

Over one hundred Black agitators marched and drove to the beginning of Little Italy, which was also the beginning of Franklin Street. Their plan was to march down it and along the way, vandalize shops and businesses with rocks and firebombs.

When the agitators arrived at the beginning of Franklin Street, they bore witness to a group of about three hundred locals: Italians, German, Polish, even Russians ready to defend their neighborhood. My dad and the Rizzo brothers were first in the group.

The locals are ready to defend their streets. But the agitators who at night would burn down certain business yelled and chanted. It was then another two hundred locals boxed them in from behind. The interlopers were outnumbered and surrounded.

One of the Rizzo Brothers casually walked over to the thugs' big-mouthed leader and had a conversation with him.

I have no idea what the exact words were, but it's fair to say with racial tensions being what they were, it was not pretty. One of the Rizzos said something to the effect of, "You Mouliyans took over what once was ours and destroyed it. You Black pieces of shit will never do that again. You aren't welcome here. Either turn your Black asses around and go back home or this will be the very place you die."

It was nothing for these big mouths to call Blacks Italian slurs like "Moulinyan," eggplant in Italian. Without hesitation the agitators turned around and left the area with a full police escort. I remember that part of the story vividly.

Years later, sometimes I would take my dates to where that standoff happened. Some things have changed in that area but the one thing that has not is the hatred that Italians have for Blacks and the feeling is mutual.

Since then, the will of the locals has been tested many times there. Back in 1979, I believe, a group of Black people tried to break into one of the shops at the beginning of Franklin Avenue, the same area where that near riot had been ten plus years before. Since they still policed that area, the local vigilantes caught them and handed out their own justice. One of the vandals was found shot in the head under a route I-91 overpass and the other two had all their fingers cut off by the vigilantes and were also later arrested. In those days the people took care of their own.

For our part, by the 1960s we had settled into normal suburban life at 22 Laurel Road. Well, as normal as it could be considering how we lived. The taxi system was up and running and, on his days off from that, my dad disappeared to the racetrack. Between this and the activity in the Clubhouse, he was putting money away again. Every weekend, there was a barbecue or some party at the house, so my mom rarely had that time for herself. Often, the only people I knew at these parties were my dad's relatives, Detective John, and his family. Newcomers were only there to talk to my dad about whatever he needed for his next project or to ask him for help with one of theirs. In that respect, it was hugely different from years before, yet somehow, it was very much the same.

On the other hand, there had also been one dramatic change.

It was no longer the three of us.

After five years of being an only child, I now had a sibling, my brother, Ralph, named after my paternal grandfather, was born shortly before we moved. My brother was my father's favorite. He was even named after my grandfather. My brother could do no wrong and became the spoiled child. My brother had frequent bouts of childhood illness. His constant need for attention was a dramatic change for my mother and me.

For me, I was no longer Dad's only son; I was just the ten-year-old "other" son. Even though I was only ten, it was evident to me that Ralph was getting all the attention while my role was reduced to absorbing the frustrations and problems life handed my father, which meant frequent spankings, which eventually progressed to the belt. By then, Geno was constantly grumpy and always yelling at my mom, especially about money and punishing me every chance he got.

My dad became downright cheap and was always complaining he was broke. This drove my mother crazy, especially since it wasn't uncommon for her to find wads of cash in his pants pockets when she did the laundry.

But this was nothing compared to how outraged she was the day she went to put something in the living room closet and accidentally found a hidden wall there.

Behind the walls were rolls of money.

Lots of rolls of money.

I mean, rolls as thick as a small log.

I got home from school that day just in time to see all the contents of the closet strewn across the living room floor, shortly after Mom made her discovery. She was working as fast as she could to put everything back before I could see, but it was too late. I saw her stuffing a roll of money back into the wall, joining the other rolls of money. There was no doubt she saw me, but she didn't say a word. She just carried on, stuffing the closet with things that were usually there: stolen cameras, our jackets, Dad's Italian winter overcoat, shoes, and whatnot.

She had long suspected Dad was just crying poor and now she had proof although she had never suspected the extent of it. And then she realized he had pretended he was close to broke just so she'd have to spend her own paycheck on household goods, food, and clothing.

It didn't occur to me until years later that for a while after she found the hiding place, she rarely complained about spending her own money on the household. I then had no doubt she had started dipping into the hidden stash until my father noticed cash was missing and found a different hiding place.

But we settled back into a normal routine for us. My parents both did their own versions of work. I went to school and my brother got dropped off at the babysitter's who lived on the same street as us. Everything was chugging along again until Mom became pregnant with my sister.

My dad was born a selfish man. The more obstacles that stood in the way between him and his desires, the meaner he got, and he had had his fair share of obstacles by the time my mother was pregnant again. Another baby meant the days of running off to Florida or Vegas certainly were over. He was going to be stuck in the suburbs with a house, a wife, three kids and major responsibilities. My mother at this time was laying down the law of the land. She had had enough and wanted my father to become a responsible adult.

There's no question another child on the way put my dad over the top. This put the lid on any and all future plans he may have had and his anger became endless. He directed this rage toward my mother and me. Later, we came to believe his undiagnosed severe depression triggered much of that. It wasn't until years later that we found out that depression was just one of his issues. My dad may have also suffered from bi-polar disease. There was a stigma to mental illness back then, especially if you were in my dad's line of work. It was believed depression was a sign of weakness and should be kept entirely secret and private.

The reasons didn't matter much to me. My ten-year reign as a spoiled only child had ended abruptly with the birth of two more children.

Our lifestyle had gotten worse, too. It wasn't terrible; it just wasn't as nice as it had been when it was just the three of us.

But the hardest part was I was old enough to know and understand a lot about what was going on. I knew for sure Dad's luck or lack thereof on anything, on any given day, would have a major bearing on his mood. The upcoming birth of my sister Gina created a terrible situation for all of us.

12. HOLIDAY IN THE EMPIRE STATE

Up until right before my sister was born, my mom was still working full-time, and all of her paycheck went into taking care of the house.

Knowing my mother was bringing in a steady income, my dad got increasingly cheaper with us and now had the perfect excuse to slack off while he planned his next big money maker. Once he had this plan, he did what any man with two children and one on the way, a faltering business and gambling habit would do. He tightened the household purse strings even more and he and his gang went to Saratoga, New York to combine their resources and buy another racehorse.

My dad loved to gamble as much, if not more, than he did running gambling games. Like any other gambler, his motivation was he would hit the big one sooner or later. That never happens to any obsessive gambler. My father was no exception and to make matters worse, he gambled big to win big and a new racehorse was another one of those gambles. This decision was unpopular with my mother, so the fact he was leaving for a few days was overall a good thing for all concerned, as tensions were high in the DiBacco home. Once Dad was gone, Rena quickly adjusted and relaxed as best as she could with us boys. She knew once he returned, he would be all bluster and excitement and full of plans like he had been with his racing dog's years earlier. She also knew that by buying the horse, she now had justification to get more money for the household. Mom had to use his time away to prepare for that battle when he got home.

And what a battle that was going to be.

As soon as Dad left, the first thing my mom did was raid his money hole. She tore into the closet only to discover the wads of cash were gone. He had taken the cash to buy a horse. That pissed her off even more.

Meanwhile, the Cadillac was speeding off to New York, full of Italian troublemakers in search of their cash cow. (Well, horse in this instance.) The Gabardine suit was safely packed in the trunk.

The Gabardine Gang was scheduled to meet up with their counterparts from Albany, NY. These guys were another group of Italians who were always looking for easy money instead of finding a safe, good paying career or job. The Albany group was made up of a mixture of Italians from all different regions in Italy, unlike my dad's group, who were all from the same region. It was their opinion, the Sicilians were slimy, low-class people and they didn't like any gang that had them as members. It's funny how mobsters can find bad in already bad people so clearly, there wasn't a lot of love between them going into the deal to begin with. A fixer out of New York City was there to broker the bids so there wouldn't be any confusion or worse, violence.

The New York gang had come into possession of eight thoroughbred horses whose previous owners had forfeited them over to cover a gambling debt. These horses were now up for sale and the New York gang had somehow been able to influence the track into letting them showcase them to prospective buyers for an entire week, something that was almost unheard of.

In my father's little network there were three groups of Italians that he stayed in contact with. They were from a few different cities: Philadelphia, Albany, Providence, New Haven, and Hartford. All the families had a mutual interest in buying and selling racehorses. Each group was nothing more than "lower level" mobsters who were in the equivalent of squires playing at the sport of kings.

Saratoga was only a 3-hour drive from Hartford, so the gang frequently went there and knew all the cheap motels and motor lodges. Dad would call home every day to check in on Mom and Mom repaid his attention by making him feel guilty for leaving us and spending all the money on this horse.

The first item on the business agenda was a trip to the stables their first morning there. The New York people had gone all out to make this an impressive event. Adjacent to the stables was a private parking area which was set aside for my dad's gang and the rest of the goombas. The hosts had security guys watching this lot full of Cadillacs.

My dad told me there were a couple of stable boys there who did nothing but wash all the cars and line them up in rows, all shiny and clean and he said there were so many cars the lot looked like a Cadillac dealership.

That morning the stables were only open to VIP gangsters and my dad and his group were included. Some members of the Rhode Island gang who Dad had known forever and occasionally worked with joined his group. They all trusted each other and felt safe together. The Albany gang was also there, and both groups immediately became interested in the first horse in the stalls in this showcase. This horse, Shadow Step, had been incredibly successful and had won some of the biggest races on the East Coast.

The hosts were aware there would be some tension between the prospective buyers, and they certainly didn't want any trouble at this extra special showcase event so there was unobtrusively present security everywhere.

This security didn't stop a fight from happening on the first day in the evening at a private event at a local lounge. Calling it a "private event" was gilding the lily a bit. Anyone seeing that many Italians driving Cadillac's and wearing nicely tailored suits and fedoras in one place knew better than to stop in uninvited. The hosts even brought in extra waitresses to make sure everyone was well taken care of during "race week." With an assembly of many well-dressed Italian men with a lot of cash and so many sexy waitresses, no one was surprised when the first fight broke out over a woman.

There's bound to be trouble when you take that many hot heads and add alcohol and pretty women.

In this case, one of the Rhode Island guys took a liking to a brunette waitress who had also caught the attention of one of the members of the Albany crew and when this rivalry couldn't be resolved with words, they "stepped out back," which in those days was the manly way to sort out your differences when words failed. In this case, "stepping out back" meant a bare knuckled one on one boxing match outside the lounge's kitchen. As crude as this mediation was, they showed respect for the host family by keeping the fight well controlled while beating the crap out of each other. Each fighter's respective gangs stood ready as backup in a moment's notice; my dad and his guy standing for the Rhode Island contender.

For their part, the host family was relatively unconcerned. With their own armed security team already in place, they were prepared for any eventuality, so they just let the guys get it out of their system.

Naturally, everyone watching this impromptu boxing match took bets on the participants.

When the fight ended, everyone shook hands and went back to the bar to drink some more.

There were two ironies that night.

The first is that neither of the guys got that girl. She left with another guy entirely.

The second was that none of the extra waitresses who had been hired, including the brunette in question, knew anything about waitressing. They were all call girls hired by the host family to make some extra money for them.

This fight had been over someone available to anyone.

It should be noted this double duty staff was an excellent business move on the hosts' part because almost every gangster had a "Goomah" or girlfriend on the side. Taking a call girl for the night was par for the course for them. (Geno never had a Goomah. He was too cheap for that!)

The auction excitement started the first night before the races. Each group of prospective buyers was given a card written in code, which detailed the days, and races each horse for sale was running in. It was done like this because the mobsters selling the horses weren't interested in the public knowing some of the races were being used to showcase their wares, so of course, there was a scheme. What they would do was register one horse in the lineup and then substitute another one of the mobsters' horses for it. For example: In the program given to the public, the horse wearing number four in the first race was named "Willie's Revenge" but one of the mob horses for sale named "Diamond Revenge" would replace it at the last minute, wearing the ringer's horse's number and colors. The ringer would always crush the other horses by as much as eight to ten lengths because they were expensive thoroughbreds running against local racehorses. The mobsters there would also use their special cards to make some extra cash betting on the ringers while also using these races to access the horsed up for sale. I never realized how smart some of these guys were. They used their wits to outsmart the system all the time.

The first day of racing went off without a hitch and Shadow Step won his race. When Dad called Mom that night, he tried to explain the gambling system he was working with, but Mom just complained about her job and then came home and had to take care of everything by herself. It was a short conversation, and I could only hear my mom's side, but I could tell he told her Shadow Step was running again in two days. That information and its importance sadly did not make an impression on her.

We waited to hear what happened. Shadow Step won his second race. The buzz Dad told my mom when he called that day that everyone knew these horses weren't regular regional racehorses. He and his guys were beginning to think they were Class A racing thoroughbreds with Kentucky lineage and even at a bargain price, they wouldn't be cheap, but the next race would be the deciding one as far as purchasing Shadow Step was concerned.

All the Italian dreamers there saw dollar signs in their dreams, and everyone was scrambling to stake their claim on their prospective horses.

This is when things got serious. Of course, everyone knew each horse would go to the highest bidder but since they were Italian, and the one thing they had in common was worshiping money, none of them wanted to spend any more than they absolutely had to. Days at the track were spent evaluating the horses and estimating what the other bids would be and at night everyone went to the homemade casino the host family threw together.

Dad said the casino the hosts put together looked like a mini-Caesars Palace and had been set up off the main floor of an old machine factory. Slot machines, roulette wheels and gaming tables were hauled in by the truckload, as were boxes of booze and dozens of pin-up model waitresses. The local police were paid off to look the other way and anyone who was bothered by all of this was simply too scared to do or say anything, even if they wanted to.

It would be almost impossible to list all my father's gambling vices, but if you were to try, somewhere close to the top would be blackjack and slot machines, slot machines having a slight edge. Dad could play the dollar slots for hours at a time even though dropping a dollar in a machine every ten seconds or so can add up quickly.

This didn't matter to him. He had a system involving slot machines where he would count the number of players on a machine and how long a particular machine took between payouts. It was a self-concocted formula he believes worked and that's what he told everyone, especially on this trip. There was no scientific evidence for this, other than my dad knew from first-hand experience that most, if not all, the slot machines in those days were easily rigged. He had done this with his own machines, so he understood how the cycles worked and how long the longest cycle was.

On one of his first nights there, he scouted a machine which was close to both the bar and the bathroom. His logic was that due to its location, this machine was going to be extremely popular. "People love to drink and then they have to pee," he'd say.

He pulled over a waitress and tucked three hundred dollars in her hand. "Watch this machine for the next couple of days when I'm not around and be sure to tell me if it hits," he told her.

She agreed and literally just sat at the bar when she was off and watched that machine for a payout and when she wasn't around; a girlfriend of hers did the same.

The machine never paid out in the three days the girls watched it, and then Geno sat and calculated. He had nothing to go on other than the hope the hosts didn't reset the cycle on the machine when it was emptied. If this happened, his entire strategy and paying off the girls to watch the machine would have been for nothing. But he was a gambler, and this kind of calculation is what he did and thought he was excellent at, despite frequent evidence to the contrary.

He knew the machines were cleaned out nightly, so he waited until the weekend races when a steady stream of people started trying their luck. The more people, the more coins were being dropped in the machine.

At the first opportunity, my dad grabbed the stool and played with his machine. He later told me he played for hours that night. He dropped around five grand into the machine when a surprise happened.

It hit and it hit big!

The machine went nuts and the floor boss came running over with a bucket. Silver dollars were flying everywhere, and Dad was grinning from ear to ear. He grabbed his waitress friend and tucked a wad of cash in her pocket. (He later said he thought in his jubilation he may have given far too much for a tip; maybe five hundred dollars or more.)

When the machine stopped, he had buckets of silver dollars, around fifty thousand dollars. It is basically a numbers game. If you can monitor a machine long enough, the odds of a payout are in your favor. My dad made fifty thousand dollars on a five-thousand-dollar investment. Geno whispered in the boss's ear who in turn signaled for an even bigger boss to come out of the back.

Dad shook his hand and then the big boss pointed for three of his guys to come over. The guys carried the coins to the window and another couple of them dragged out a cart to put the slot machine in and they wheeled the machine out the door.

My dad had bought the slot machine to take home and put it in the Clubhouse.

This entire transaction was very illegal to say the least. He grabbed his cash and tucked it nicely into a leather case, then walked out to his Cadillac where his guys and the casino people were throwing the three-hundred-pound behemoth slot machine into the trunk. The next day he took the guys out to the nearest steak house and with his new winnings, spent five hundred dollars on dinner.

As far as the horse auction went, every horse there had multiple bidders and buyers. My dad's new winnings pretty much locked in the horse they wanted, as he had an extra $50,000 dollars to play with. My dad and his guys got the horse that they wanted, won a little money, and didn't get into too many fights.

My dad considered this to be an extraordinarily successful trip. It was a different story when my dad came home and had to answer to my mom.

About a month after that trip, he received the bill for boarding and training Shadow Step. This bill was a new household bill in the name of the horse's new legal owner, my dad.

When my mom caught a glimpse of what it cost to board this racehorse, you would have thought World War Three just started. We were scrimping and saving as it was, and that bill was hundreds of dollars a month.

My mom was livid.

My dad just did what he did best: ignored her and walked away.

This was an ongoing problem between them for many years, they were terrible at communicating.

They either got along fine or argued and there was not much of a middle ground there this time.

13 WHEELS AND PELOTAS IN WINDSOR LOCKS

A couple of months had passed after he got home from his Saratoga Spree and Dad was still trying to get back on my mom's good side. The monthly bills for his latest acquisition didn't help with the thaw. For the most part, she gave him the cold shoulder, which was the only consistently cold thing around our miserably hot home that summer.

My poor Mom was seven or eight months pregnant with my sister and miserable from that and the summer heat while my dad was getting increasingly cheaper. He would only put on the air conditioning in the big playroom we had in the garage which was his main hangout at home. This left the kitchen and living room, where Mom spent most of her time, frequently sweltering.

One exceptionally sweltering day, Dad decided we all needed ice cream. How bad can a dad be who takes you out for ice cream? He can still be a pretty bad dad as I learned later that day.

I know he began that Saturday with good intentions. Selfish as always, but good. However, all the good intentions in the world couldn't stop what happened that day.

The four of us loaded into the Cadillac and headed to Hartford for ice cream. Dad had to make everything a big deal so instead of just going down the road to the local shop like normal people, we had to drive ten miles to his favorite place.

It started out as a fun ride. Johnny Cash was on the radio, the car windows were wide open, my brother and I were in the back seat, and no one was wearing seat belts as they weren't mandatory like they are today. Dad merged onto the highway and off we went down Interstate 91.

Suddenly, some guy in a Pontiac raced up to my dad's bumper and in his rush to take the next exit, which was just a little bit ahead of us, he cut us off. Thinking quickly

My dad slammed on the brakes, thrusting us all forward and nearly jolting Ralph and I out of our seat.

My mom just screamed and turned around to us, reaching her arm back to make sure we didn't get thrown into the front seat.

We were at a dead stop in the middle of the highway while that dumbass drove down the exit like a madman.

No one said a word.

Dad looked at Mom. She nodded and said, "They're okay."

He gunned the Cadillac and that big V8 engine revved up and made the distinct roar those cars always made once they're fully opened up. From our places in the back seat, between the speed and the sound, Ralph and I almost thought we were in a rocket.

My mom looked back at us sheepishly as if to say, "You guys shouldn't be seeing this," and then she turned back around, adjusted her headscarf but still didn't say a word. The Cadillac went from zero to sixty in seconds, and we jumped off at the same exit as that other driver. He blew through the stop sign and set sail after the dumbass.

We were now in Windsor, home of The Clubhouse and coincidentally, the town the cops were paid off in, so traffic violations weren't going to be an issue. It only took a few miles for my dad to catch up to this jackass who had been driving erratically all the way down the street. Mom made us put on our seat belts. My dad was going so fast trees were moving outside my window like they were only feet apart.

Mom, who has seen this type of behavior many times before, managed to hold back her tears and yelled. "Geno, just to let it go," but my Dad was possessed.

My mom knew what was on the other end for this guy if my dad caught him.

Geno knew this town and all its streets like the back of his hand. We went down some side streets and a few long roads to a secluded part of town where he knew the main road that fool was on ended up.

My dad caught up to this guy who clearly was drunk. Geno raced in front of his car and cut him off so he couldn't get by. The Pontiac was pinned between our Cadillac and some trees on the side of the road.

Mom looked back at us.

"This is none of your business. Just keep quiet and eat this fruit," she said, handing us both an apple.

"Kev, behave and keep an eye on your brother."

She didn't say I couldn't peek over the seat, which of course I did, so I saw my dad bolt out of the Cadillac and run over to the other driver's door. The driver's window was open and the look on this guy's face was one of shock and fear. He recognized our car and was already apologizing as my dad came towards him. My dad, all five foot eight of angry Italian in full fury, reached into the window and grabbed the driver by both shoulders. He literally dragged these six feet two, two-hundred-pound guy through the window of his car and onto the ground. Dad clocked him in the face a couple of times, knocking him groggy. Then, he dragged him about ten yards into the thick trees on the side of the road. That's all I could see from the back window.

It was then that my spying was caught.

Mom reached back and pushed me down in my seat.

"Kev, mind your own business. This doesn't concern you," she said.

Moments later, my dad returned to the car, his Banlon polo shirt now bloody. He was sweating, but he had a semi smile on his face.

Mom's eyes were glued on him, waiting for him to say something, when he jumped back into the Cadillac. I knew she feared my dad might have killed that drunk.

After a few minutes he said to Mom, "What?"

He paused for a second and then continued.

"No, I didn't."

He seemed puzzled.

"He'll be fine. A few broken bones, that's all," he continued, and that statement concluded things as far as he was concerned.

Mom exhaled a deep sigh of relief and fell back into the car seat and Dad grabbed a towel from her. We always had towels on hand because I was a slob and was always spilling food in the Cadillac. He wiped his face and shirt the best he could and continued down the road to the ice cream shop.

When we got to the ice cream stand, Mom knew going to the window was going to be her job, as Dad was a bloody mess. He threw her some cash and told her he'd like a chocolate dipped vanilla cone.

We sat there for twenty minutes and ate our ice cream. It was like nothing happened and no one said a word about it. From that point on, I was afraid to question my dad about anything (by now, you know I'm always full of questions) and the worst part is, he only got meaner and more questionable from then on.

After the ice cream adventure, my dad's attempts to get back into my mom's good graces were pretty much limited to staying out of her hair. He drove the taxi part time and went to the track the rest of the time. Connecticut's newly created gambling commission made it even easier for him to blow his money when a new "off track betting" (OTB) system set up shop in Hartford.

Geno was in heaven.

He was no longer limited to reports from the track or the radio and could watch horse races from tracks in New York, New Jersey, and all around the east coast on the dozens of televisions that were the staple of OTB establishments. He would meet the guys there to have lunch and watch their horses run. It was perfect for them. Big New York trips were no longer necessary.

On slow days, Dad found himself driving passengers for Patel and he liked the fact his cash tips could be pocketed and used at the OTB. My dad was barely doing anything else to make money. Dad always had to find a scheme to make money. It wasn't in his blood to work a conventional type of job for twenty years. My dad was always looking for a quick make money scam.

More forward-looking people than my father, like my mother for example, could have predicted societal changes were going to make my father's business model in need of a substantial business makeover if not totally obsolete. The unpredicted births of not one, but two children arriving five years apart weakens the Geno-centric culture that he had created. In his mind his empire began to collapse. That only added to our financial instability.

He had always known things for him business-wise were going to change a lot when we moved.

When I look back on it now, I'm sure that was a big part of the reason he and my mother fought so much about moving. It would be easy to write off his stubbornness as just part of his arrogant, selfish nature but all those flaws aside, one thing my father wasn't was stupid and I've always thought he could have done quite well in a legitimate profession, Although he probably never admitted it to my mother, I'm convinced he feared moving because he feared losing his universe and having to create a new one.

Dangling Man had been the first major sign our universe was going to implode on itself. It hadn't been just because this Moulinyan had been drunk and stupid enough to break into our home.

It was a complete disrespect to my father and the way of life he had built for my mother and me. Dangling Man had broken into, and effectively torn down, the wall around us my dad had so carefully built as well as my father's entire way of making a living and providing for his family.

Since we now lived too far away from Hartford for my dad to oversee the heists and fencing, he let his guys control more and more of that part of the action and this led to less income for him. With the sale of Pal's, the Little Casino was gone; he no longer had the prostitutes in their apartment in our building earning money for him; our move out of the neighborhood meant he had relinquished his authority in the protection racket and my mom had forced him out of his small chain of illegal abortion clinics. All these changes meant my dad was easily running less than half the operations and therefore making much less money than he had when he was at the top of his game.

My dad was cheap and sneaky, so my mom's best guess was to piece together the money he and the Gabardine Gang were making in their hay day per month: 10K gambling; 5-10K loan sharking and another 5-10K moving stolen products, the latter being inconsistent because the shipments themselves were. Twenty-five thousand a month in 1962 was a LOT of money. After our move from Hartford and the near split from his guys, he was lucky to bring in 1-2K a month.

Plus, to say he got lazy would be an understatement and gambling became his obsession more than ever. His laziness paled in comparison to his gambling addiction.

"Do what you love," is often given as career advice, and while being a mobster isn't a traditional career path, the same adage can apply.

Mobsters like making easy money.

That's the main reason why they are in that profession. And this professional interest in money often puts them in close proximity to gambling; both running it and doing it. There is money to be made gambling (theory) and running gambling operations (fact). My dad liked both, although he was more partial to the former than the latter.

The thrill of gambling has crushed many people both in and out of the mob. Even the great New York Gangster Arnold Rothstein, who many people still believe had a hand in fixing the 1919 World Series, couldn't control his gambling obsession and it led to his downfall and my father was on the same path.

My dad fancied himself a successful gambler, particularly after his big slot machine win, but if he won twenty percent of the time, which would be a high estimate. To make matters worse, my dad wasn't a casual weekend type of gambler. He never threw down less than a hundred dollars on a horse and he always played the win and would "box" the horse to Win/Place/Show, meaning he had bets on all three of these options for just one horse, but on a good day with all his inside information, he could win 4-5K. On a bad day, my dad would lose a thousand dollars easily.

Don't get me wrong.

It wasn't that he wasn't making any money. If he had just put the money he spent on gambling into the household, we would have all been fine and probably could have continued in our Barbour Street lifestyle, even with two more children in the house.

But his selfishness and obsession were just too great and that was what upset my mom the most. She didn't know how to change his behavior or open his eyes as to what was happening to our family other than to keep the pressure on him to earn more. She knew the leopard wasn't going to change its spots, so in her eyes, pressuring him to bring home more money was the only viable solution.

My father was always looking for a quick buck and one day while driving his little taxi all over the city he stumbled upon a sure-fire way to rip people off.

On that day, he was asked to pick up a group of visiting professors from out west at the airport and bring them to the college.

It wasn't just any college; it was the Connecticut Institute for the Blind.

My dad was all over it.

In this case, the foundation for an evil plan just fell into his lap. And he knew exactly what he had to do to make what would usually be an average fare highly profitable.

The three blind professors he picked up were unaccompanied. The school trusted my dad would get them there in one piece. These poor visitors were at his mercy and had no idea who they were dealing with.

This ride was on a windy fall day and my dad got them to the college safely. You might think blind people would have a problem paying with cash but that was not the case. To prevent them from getting robbed, they had a system worked out so they could tell what the denominations of different bills in their wallet were. It had something to do with the bills having different feels and textures.

As luck would have it, the wind was gusting so hard that day that as one of the professors pulled out his wallet to pay my dad, its contents went flying. Bills and travelers checks all blew into a nearby puddle. My father, always the opportunist, played Mr. Nice Guy and ran over to gather all the money for them. They thought he was a saint. The professor, in his panicked state, was overjoyed my dad had been a real humanitarian who hadn't taken advantage of this situation.

My dad had successfully taken five hundred dollars for a fourteen-dollar cab fare from a group of blind professors.

The bills were wet, making it impossible for the blind man to tell what the amounts were. By the time the school administrators came out to greet their guests, my dad had thoroughly ripped them off, helped the professor get his money back in his wallet and was acting like a hero. The professor, not knowing what had happened to him, tucked his wallet back in his pocket and he and his colleagues praised my dad for being a stand-up guy. Not only did this reveal how low my dad would go to generate money, but it also started a new business model for him.

Picking up blind clients.

They never knew what hit them.

Thrilled at his new score, my father spent that afternoon betting at the expense of these poor, blind visiting professors. He blew their five hundred dollars at an OTB and never told anyone but me that story.

Meanwhile, my mom was counting down the days for my sister to be born. She'd had enough of being late term in her pregnancy at the peak of summer. She also knew that another mouth to feed would really have to make her motivate my father to get his shit together and be active in home life.

Of all the changes I witnessed as a child, my sister's birth had the biggest effect on my father's behavior.

At first, he was a proud papa of a baby girl named Gina, after Gina Lollobrigida, a famous Italian actress. He would show her off to everyone and she sure was an attention grabber the first few months of her life. But Dad's excitement with having a baby daughter wore off within a year or two. After that, he decided Gina was a mistake and no longer wanted anything to do with her. When he did see her, he would ridicule her which made her feel terrible. At an early age, my sister was made to cry by my father the bully. She was just a child.

We never really knew why he had this change of heart about her and to this day, we haven't been able to put a finger on it.

Once my sister was born, everything changed for him. He became more reclusive, less able to deal with people, and he pulled away from many of his friends and once again, he pulled away from me too. Gone were the days of little

Kevy being the pampered child and the center of attention in my universe. It was a harbinger of what I was going to go through in the next years.

The first months of my sister's infancy consumed my mom and dad. My mom wanted my father to take on more responsibility and she was deadly serious about that. She laid down some rules and expected him to get his shit together in a timely fashion. This was going to mean a lot of changes but primarily his unique methods of fencing items, running his books, and playing with the horses. He needed a complete lifestyle makeover if my mother was ever going to be happy again.

Our household was full of chaos and turmoil. Mom had quit her job at the plant; having two babies plus me was more than enough to keep her busy and my dad was not coming through emotionally or financially for us. Things were quickly eroding at 22 Laurel Road. My parents argued constantly, much more than I ever remembered. I would take my brother to the park when it looked like there was going to be a major war and, in those days, we spent a lot of time there.

One of the first things on my mom's list of demands was the racehorse. She insisted my dad sell his share of Shadow Step and stop this expensive obsession. (Just room and board was hundreds of dollars a month. There were to be no more stable and boarding fees and certainly no more trips to lose money gambling on that horse. While I wasn't home the day that battle happened, I knew my mother won that one by using some serious scare tactics including threatening to expose to the authorities how he had managed to launder all his money over the years. My dad simply had to bow to her insistence he stop pissing money away, at least in this instance. Dad sold his share of Shadow Step to his guys, and they assumed all the associated expenses.

My mom may have won that battle, but my dad was dead set on winning the war. This was the first conflict of many which contributed to the total erosion of my parents' relationship.

Looking back, I don't know how my mom stayed with my dad for so long other than she had the patience of a saint. My memories of my father being fun are far outweighed by my memories of those of his indifference and cruelty. He was selfish, arrogant, and only really cared about his own agenda. Everyone around them knew this about him and knew things had to change in our family or the DiBacco clan was doomed.

This didn't seem to bother him at all.

As long as he was taking care of himself, feeding his gambling addiction, Geno had no problem sleeping at night. He simply didn't care we were struggling as he enjoyed himself.

His antics were covering a deeper issue, his health. My dad's health had taken a turn for the worse as well. His diabetes had a grip on him, he began to lose his eyesight in one eye and his circulation was very bad in his legs and feet.

My mom intuitively knew something was wrong with him other than his characteristic lack of empathy. She finally succeeded in nagging him enough to go to the doctor and the diagnosis was type-1 diabetes and he had to go on a daily insulin regimen. He also had to slow his pace down, although he stayed as active as he could and busy enough to provide the necessities for us, although it was marginal after what I had always known. In another small concession to my mother, he traveled to The Clubhouse less frequently and made fewer trips to the OTB.

All of this was quite a lifestyle change for him in the ten years since I had been born.

I have always believed all this change led to him suffering from depression, which in those days was pretty much both unmentionable and untreatable with medication like we have today. In addition, my father was the last person in the world who would go to a shrink. Discussing his problems or feelings with a stranger was simply unthinkable to him and no one would have dared suggest it.

For her part, my mom was always smoother and did her best to fix things herself and work out her problems with my dad. She never backed down from her responsibilities to her family even when more than her share of the work was thrust upon her.

The taxi system ran fine for quite some time because Dad and his gang still had some of the heisting and fencing infrastructure still in place. The only thing that was different from the Barbour Street days was the addition of using the cabs to shuttle stolen merchandise and cash around. And then trouble struck Patel, who was busted by immigration. The INS investigation of him slowed down the entire system my dad had put into place.

My father was livid the day INS agents came to our front door to talk to him about Patel and his taxi business. Federal agents showing up at your front door can unnerve anyone, my dad included. When he learned they were INS, he was puzzled. This agency had no reason or jurisdiction to speak to him about his sideline operation from the taxis, not that they suspected it or would have cared even if they did know. Their only interest in illegal activity was people getting into the country without going through the proper channels. When he learned the agents were only interested in Patel, who they believed had forged his citizenship papers in order to open his taxi business, my father was furious.

Patel, being in jeopardy put his sideline business in jeopardy as well.

Plus, he wasn't stupid. Patel's business was going very well, and he was pretty sure a competitor had ratted Patel out to the INS.

The INS agents were kind and polite. They talked to my dad for an hour that night and my mom served them coffee and homemade chocolate cake. (If you ever ate a slice of one of my mom's homemade cakes, you would quickly forget about everything else.) From what I could hear from the other end of the house, the conversation eventually became lighter, and I was never sure what they wanted to learn from my dad. He had never been a formal employee of Patel's and from what I can remember, he never left a paper trail on any of those jobs or transactions he did.

That was one consistent thing about him. He excelled at keeping a low profile and never leaving a paper trail. I don't have any photos of him and any members of the gang or their associates together.

These photos weren't lost or destroyed.

They never existed.

Once the agents left the house, I could tell my dad was furious. I wasn't sure if he was mad at Patel for being illegal or because his smuggling system was going to be interrupted. Of course, as things turned out, he didn't give a rat's ass if Patel was going to get deported; he had got what he needed from him. My dad was far more upset because his revenue stream was in danger of taking a hit. Against another wall, he had to scramble to fix this situation as quickly as possible in order to limit any interruptions to his operation. After all, this was still a very large part of his income. My mom was curious to see how he was going to handle this. He didn't have time to waste to come up with a solution, but he also knew the Feds worked slowly so he had some leeway to come up with a long-range plan instead of a quick fix.

In this instance, my mother had faith in my father. She had seen him get in and out of jams for so long and so often she figured he would find a way, particularly because he knew and had paid off so many people in high places. And in this case, her faith in him was not misplaced, although since it was my father, it came with a unique twist.

While the Patel saga with the Feds dragged on, he just kept running his angle on the taxicab business right under the Fed's noses, an act that was both arrogant and fearless. It might also have been called stupid, were it not for the fact that nothing ever happened to him or any member of his gang.

Ever.

Not in this situation with the taxis and him being on the radar of the feds.

Not on the close call that almost cost Sonny his life.

Not one brush with authorities over the millions of laundered monies that passed through his gambling operations and other business ventures.

During the time my dad and the Gabardine Gang controlled all organized crime in Hartford, which was well over a decade, they never once got into trouble for any of the illegal things they did.

By now, stories about mobsters thinking they are untouchable are well known and it's easy to conclude my father was another one of those guys. He certainly was arrogant enough for it and it would not be a stretch to assume this was another one of his many character flaws.

However, he had one thing going for him that all the famous, fallen mobsters you've heard of, did not.

He was not in the least bit famous, or infamous, for that matter.

He was just one of the hundreds, if not thousands of minor league crime bosses scattered throughout America. Unless they made a huge mistake or someone ratted them out, the authorities really didn't care about them back then. Simply put, trying to take them down was more bother than it was worth.

Not to mention that from the perspective of their communities and the people in authority these types of mobsters dealt with daily, they were providing a service overall. People on a budget could get high end goods for next to nothing compared to what it would have cost them retail. The free lunches and perks he gave to the police at the Game Room, Little Casino and later, Willie's and The Clubhouse were enough to keep them off his back, and the value of his long-standing friendship with Detective John cannot be underestimated. Plus, the presence of him and the gang as they self-policed the neighborhood meant the cops could concentrate on crime in other neighborhoods. Most other public officials who might have been concerned about his activities found their interest diverted with a wink and a moneyed handshake.

This wasn't unique to my dad; this was status quo for all minor league mobsters.

Of course, you're wondering what the big-league guys thought about them. Frankly, they simply didn't care much as long as they didn't interfere with major business and they could be counted on to lend a hand if they were called on, which happened in only a small capacity and very rarely.

Bottom line, they were a very small operation relatively speaking and took care (one way or the other) of everyone who could take them down.

And now that you have a better idea about how my dad's operation worked, you will understand how this applied to the Great Taxi Scam.

Detective John kept my father updated as to what was going on with the investigation into Patel. The feds worked closely with the Hartford detectives and John was able to get updates on the case as it went along. This gave my dad a ballpark idea of when the shit was going to hit the fan.

Patel's taxi operation, both the legitimate side as well as my father's more unsavory side continued for months until the Feds had enough information to shut the business down, confiscate the cabs and go about the business of deporting Patel. My dad was fully prepared for this, as everyone thought he would be since he had plenty of lead-time to construct his backup plan. My mother wasn't easily surprised by anything he ever did but this scheme caught her totally off guard when he unveiled it in his usual abrupt way.

My dad's foolproof plan was to start his own taxi business.

My mother's jaw hit the floor when he proposed the idea. "Proposed" isn't the right word.

He came home one day and laid out his new business model.

Rena had been telling him for months she wanted to save money and his plan was to spend more money on another dumbass venture he already had the wheels in motion for.

He had bought a new Plymouth Fury to start his own taxi business and he was going to have fitted with the identical storage unit he had in Patel's cabs. As far-fetched as this scheme was, Mom knew he had to keep what little of his businesses he had left and to her credit, she wholeheartedly helped him start up his taxi business.

He went to the state regulations board and got all the paperwork and forms to start Geno's Taxi. There were mounds of paperwork my mom helped him with. Between the new car, the licensing, insurances, and getting the meter system installed he easily spent a few thousand dollars.

My dad's taxi was the world-wide debut of a portable mobster front for illegal activity.

Usually mobsters used restaurants, bars, butcher shops, body shops and other standard businesses to run their illegal operations out of. Balancing an illegal operation on the back of a legal business isn't easy although I've always thought there must be some sort of mobster handbook to learn this trick. My dad was good at doing this, at first with Pal's and now the taxi business. To pull off The Great Taxi Scam, he would have to operate his taxi like any other taxi business: pick up people, log his fares and run meter reports.

Many of his friends thought he was crazy. After all, he really disliked the public and at some point, was going to have to interact with them.

At this point, knowing what you know about Geno, you are guessing he had another angle to his new taxi business other than simply installing a false bottom in his cab to transport stolen merchandise and occasionally ripping off blind people and you would be correct. Not one to ever take the conservative route and with the help of Henry and David, he also introduced meter tampering.

This was very tricky. All of the regulations for running a public transportation business are regulated by the state and it's a very difficult system to skirt. But my dad wasn't one to shirk from a challenge, especially if it involved easy money, so his plan was to make his taxi unlike any other.

To that end, he paid off the state public transportation board.

Not the entire board of course, just the two people who were critical to this new venture: the person who installed the meter and the meter inspector, who he already knew. Once this was done, he ended up with a unique meter in his taxi.

You see, a meter is an extraordinarily complex machine which is connected to the odometer of a car. It has a set rate per mile, registers the mileage for each fare, including the minimum mileage charge and the total amount charged for each fare. My dad's special meter registered a nickel more per mile.

"A Nickel," you say. "No big deal."

Doesn't sound like much, but these taxis logged at least a couple thousand miles a week.

And in today's money, that was about six thousand dollars a week in just that extra nickel.

On the surface, my dad was running a "by the book" company every day. And only three people knew he was ripping off the system with both a rigged meter and often stashes of stolen goods in the trunk of his taxi. It was quite a racket. The working way to make money on this rigged meter was to actually use the taxi for business, although my dad was never big on working the hard way.

And that was the catch. This would be a great scheme if you were a normal cab driver working forty or fifty hours a week, picking up any who flagged you down. Just like that extra nickel a mile on every trip adds up, those extra trips add up too. Dad used his expensively rigged and "bought off" meter as little as possible for jobs like that. He was a creature of habit and, as it's been noted, not much of a "people person."

My dad wasn't about to change his routine. His daily work schedule included trips to the track, OTB, and other gambling venues.

Unlike regular, hardworking taxi drivers, he would freelance and pick up only select people, usually those who looked like they could tip well, although he did manage to get some regular clients.

His first regular customer was the same school for the blind where he had scored big only months earlier. They loved my dad for what he did. In their estimation, he was a hero for recovering the professor's money. What they didn't know was that he was constantly ripping their people off.

The hospital was another favorite spot for my dad to camp out. The doctors and nurses were all paid well and as a result, they tipped well too.

He also made frequent stops at Bradley International Airport. On a few occasions, Dad picked up legendary Hollywood movie star Katherine Hepburn and brought her to her home in West Hartford. In those days, she frequently flew back and forth from Connecticut to California. He also taxied around people like Bob Seger, Peter Faulk, Charles Nelson Riley, the Allman Brothers, Tina Turner, Dionne Warwick, and dozens of other celebrities who flew into Hartford. My dad liked to say he became the taxi for the stars. All the time, while there were celebrities in the back seat, he had a trunk full of stolen guns or jewels with their own destinations.

His goal was to reach for the money and only be in situations where it was economically sound for him and that's what he did. As that was his position, my dad rarely went into the North End with his taxi business, or any impoverished areas for that matter, although he would stop in to visit the old neighborhood to say hi to his friends who still ran businesses there.

From my father's perspective, life was just one pressure-filled downward spiral. First it was the pressure to move, and when my brother spent his first few months in and out of the hospital with multiple ear infections. My mother applied was the pressure to change and rebuild his business and put us back in the lifestyle we had always enjoyed before my brother was born and we moved to the suburbs and away from the hub of his universe. Then when my sister was born five years later, my father felt like that was the end of his gangster days.

Geno felt sorry for himself, about the pressure he was under and those factors, combined with his intractable selfishness and gambling addiction meant he didn't spend less on himself, he just cut back on money for the family, which now included three children.

My brother didn't notice the change in our household. He was too young to remember anything about our lifestyle on Barbour Street, and Gina of course, had never known it, but I wasn't.

Life in the North End had been noisy and fun.

I had Dotty and Jinx for company and Sonny to carry me around the neighborhood on his shoulders. We ate out all the time, Dad was always buying my mom expensive gifts and me, pretty much anything I wanted. It was a far cry from how we were living now. I had watched my father go from king of the hill, with multiple operations, new Cadillacs, fancy clothes, vacations three times a year and more, to almost nothing.

My mom set up rules and he was expected to live by them. Sensible rules, "Don't waste all your money on gambling" and "Three kids mean you need to make more money." He always said he was trying to do the right thing, but his words were always louder than his actions.

Having been married to him for over ten years, my mother knew that as far as promises to his family went, especially ones he felt pressured into making, only a serious threat would get him to back down. She hadn't forgotten it took Mumma and her shotgun in Maine to get him to commit to moving out of Hartford. She had no problem telling Dad she would take all of us kids back up there if he didn't tow her line and he certainly didn't want to see the business end of Grandma's shotgun again.

I don't know if my parents still loved each other deep down by then. I know they weren't the same parents they were when I was five or six. There was no passion in their marriage, and they seemed to stay together out of habit and for us.

While my mother had always wanted more children, I think it's safe to say she didn't plan on having two of them so much later than me, especially my sister, who is ten years younger. And then of course, she still had me to raise, and I was growing up fast.

I never for a moment doubted my mother still loved me very much, but even though I was only eleven, I was old enough to understand I was low on her priority list. On top of us kids, she had a husband with an unsteady, illegal income and a steady bad temper which made managing a household challenging to say the least.

Returning to her job at the plant was impossible with the three of us. The only thing she could do was make do the best she could with what money my dad brought home and keep up the pressure on him for more money. This pressure wasn't unreasonable. Even if he had simply used his fancy taxi meter system to actually pick up passengers, she probably would have been happy with that little bit of extra money and frankly, just knowing he was trying harder.

That small compromise, picking up fares as part of his taxi driver description didn't fit in well with my dad's work ethic and personality. Unlike his brothers who worked long hours in their trades, my father rarely worked a forty-hour week. Plus, between his depression and diabetes, working harder was simply more difficult. His frustrations grew exponentially as his failure, and my mother's pressure, increased and like all pressure, it needed an outlet. It was totally against his limited morals to do anything untowardly to my mother. My brother was by now the designated favorite child and was spared any punishment from my father as he was frequently sick, and my sister was always held up in her room far away from my father. As for Dad and me, the older I got, the less we got along. My father would bring home weekly toys for my brother, take him out for ice cream while my friends and I were at the park. When he got home, he would bark out orders for me. Sometimes it was cleaning the gutters, raking the yard, hand till the garden. Any type of manual labor came my way, while my brother played inside with his new gifts. There was no question that my dad was showing off his little Italian boy to the world.

Every building pressure needs an outlet or else whatever is pressurized will explode. Pressure was certainly rising in the DiBacco household, and an explosion was imminent.

But until that time, that left me to be the pressure valve in the house and as a result, I became my father's scapegoat and personal handyman.

It didn't take long after my dad went into the taxi business before I was handed daily chores. I don't mean chores like picking up my room or mowing the yard. At eleven years old, I was appointed maintenance man and personal servant of Geno DiBacco. My first assignment was to wash and vacuum the cab every night by hand and make sure it was clean for the next day.

Every day, winter, summer, spring, and fall.

Imagine my friends' looks when they would come over to play ball and I had no choice but to tell them I couldn't because I had to work.

All of my friends knew that I could be relegated to a manual labor task at any time. My friends in the neighborhood knew my dad was the mean old taxi driving bastard of Laurel Road.

I didn't have a say about my entree into automobile maintenance nor did I ever get an allowance for my work like kids do today. My father's thinking was I was old enough to pull my weight and since my mom was working him, he was going to work me. The more cantankerous he got, the harder I had to work for him.

I became my dad's handyman and the bigger I developed physically, the more work he piled on me while also keeping me under a strict curfew and constant fear of screwing up. Life at home was no picnic and my mom and I cherished the time when Dad was away. When he was home, he became a drill sergeant.

Cleaning the taxi every day was just part of my duties. As the months passed, if my father was home, he would always find other projects for me to work on. Building sheds or fences around the yard, chopping down trees, building cement sidewalks and tilling the garden. You name it and I had to do it by myself. In the winter, there was also snow shoveling. I was certainly fed up with being the household maintenance man at only eleven years old.

My mom really had no power in what my dad did, as long as he didn't punch me, other than in my arm. Corporeal punishment was commonplace then, even the belt, which he started to use regularly on me when I was twelve, was pretty normal, although using the buckle end was considered a bit much even then. Today that would be called child abuse, back them it was called the Italian way of keeping you in line.

She was concerned about this of course, but back then, it was something you took in stride, nothing you called the cops about. To mitigate this, she tried to make sure she never pointed out mistakes I had made when Dad was around. She just watched in disbelief most times. Mom knew my dad was nothing like he used to be. She monitored the situation between him and me very closely and they battled like the two stubborn people they both were when she thought my dad had been too strict in his approach with me.

My dad was adept at verbal abuse and his anger escalated each time I made even the slightest mistake. In his mind, I became a whipping post. He was always on me with verbal assaults: calling me a loser; telling me that I was going to be a big dumb stunad, or I'd amount to shit.

That was bad, but things took a turn for the worse one day in 1969 that literally signaled life was going to be more different for me compared to that of my friends than I had ever imagined.

A whistle I heard from the far side of the house changed everything for me that day.

My father had decided he would invent a distinctive two fingered whistle to summon me when he wanted me. The problem was he never told me what this odd whistle had to do with me.

I heard a second whistle. There was a small pause then I heard yelling.

It came closer and I realized it was my father.

"Did you hear my whistle, you big buffoon?" my dad yelled at me.

"When you hear that whistle, you drop everything and get your fat ass to me quickly, you useless stunade," he continued, shouting at the top of his lungs.

My mother heard his yelling and came running over.

"Geno, what the Hell is going on?" she asked loudly.

My dad turned to her and shouted, "When I whistle, I want that big buffoon to come running."

My mom said, "You don't whistle for your son, you stupid son of a bitch!"

My dad turned to her and said, "Shut your goddamn mouth. He'll do what I say."

He then turned to me, "And you, gavone, get your dumb ass over to the driveway" as he pulled off his belt.

I remember those few minutes that flashed past like yesterday. It was when my life changed forever. That whistle was used for me until I turned eighteen, which was when Geno said I became an adult. If I had any remaining hopes of once again becoming a coddled child, that ended the day my dad whistled for me like a dog, and like a dog, when I failed to obey, I was struck with his belt on the first of what would be far too many times.

My dad began treating me worse than his lowest crew members and my life became a childhood nightmare.

As the next few months rolled along, I realized I was doomed. My dad did everything he could to distance himself from the family and handing out chores for me was just one of those. He found another way to accomplish this when a new Jai Alai facility opened in Hartford.

If this sport is as unfamiliar to you as it was to me at first, Jai Alai is similar to racquetball or handball, and it's played on a court twice as long as a racquetball court. Single players or doubles teams use baskets or "cestas'," which looks like a short, curved Lacrosse stick to throw the ball against the wall. The sport was new to the Northeast but was huge in Florida and Latin America. It was a legal gambling sport like horse or dog racing had become with the introduction of OTB and quickly became another betting outlet for my dad and his guys. Always up for a new "get rich" scheme. The gang really thought that they could make it rich off of Jai Alai.

This new vice was about to touch off a war back home.

Of course, this being a gambling activity, my dad got in on the ground floor and met many of the Jai Alai players and their owners. The players were professionals who were backed by businesses and individuals. Yes, you guessed it, my dad, knowing he could own a piece of the action, met a couple of players from Columbia looking for backers and decided he and the guys would help finance them.

One night he came home from the fronton, the venue where Jai Alai is played, in a great mood. I don't think I had ever heard words (unless they were expletives) as "Jai Alai" used so much one night in our household.

First, Geno made a big deal out of giving Ralph and me a couple of cesta and pelotas, the game balls used in that sport. We thought this equipment was very cool.

He also gave my mother some cash and told her he was making money at the games. She didn't think how he had gotten the cash, was very cool at all and was less than thrilled he had found another gambling outlet, but the money he brought home that night momentarily appeased her.

While I'm sure sponsoring these players wasn't as costly as owning a racehorse, these guys had to travel all over South America as part of their circuit and paying for those kinds of expenses could not have been cheap.

For the first time in my vocation as a super spy kid, I was never able to overhear any conversations about how the Jai Alai angle worked for my dad and his guys. I don't know how much money was spent or how much money they made (or lost).

My father was wising up to the fact that talking about business around the house (me) would always somehow get back to my mom. I do know he and the guys went every Saturday for a year or two until they stopped going regularly.

I can only guess they lost a hefty chunk of money. Even obsessive gamblers know how to change their bets after enough losses. That must have happened with my dad and Jai Alai.

14. NO HOLIDAY IN THE NUTMEG STATE

By the time I was twelve, I began to be treated like an indentured servant in the House of DiBacco. I had to do low-level work like the grunts or wannabes in my dad's gang had always done before we moved, and my life became a childhood nightmare.

My responsibilities had expanded to some basic mechanics: replacing and rotating tires, changing the oil, and doing all other repairs I was capable of at my age. By then, Ralph was old enough not to need my mother's constant supervision, so she passed that chore on to me. When I did get some free time, I had to take Ralph with me, which I resented as I got older.

My father was getting worse in every respect.

He continued to lose his battle with depression and diabetes, on top of that, he still had all the pressures from both my mother about the household finances and from his uncontrollable, obsessive gambling.

At least he wasn't a drunk. I can't imagine what life would have been like if he were an alcoholic as well. He was short-fused and always angry and once he crossed over the line from verbal abuse to the belt after the whistle incident, the belt became his tool of choice for his frequent and self-justified discipline of me.

"Your grandfather did this to me when I was your age," he'd say to me. "Every kid in the neighborhood got the belt at home. Don't be such a vigliacco."

I didn't know if what he told me about his childhood neighborhood was true. What I did know was none of my friends were punished as hard or as often as me. I also knew my brother was exempt from any type of discipline. As mean as my father was, he would never strike a five-year-old with a belt, but I don't remember Ralph ever getting spanked or even yelled at for anything he did. My sister was never seen. She literally spent all her time at home in her bedroom or playing at her friends. My sister's goal was to stay far away from my father. She only had to deal with him at mealtime, then would retreat to her safe space.

My mother was quickly trying to figure out how to get out of this situation. Mom had many friends, and she was loved by all. She was constantly asking her friends what their home life was like, how their kids were being treated. For me I would get the belt for just talking back to my father. If I touched something of his, I would get the belt harder than for any other infraction. This sent my mom into a rage trying to protect me.

Despite all of this, from the time I was eleven until my early teens, I was always trying to impress my dad and give him something to be proud of. When I was eleven, I decided to compete in the local punt, pass and kick competition in our area. My dad took a sudden interest in this competition but of course, too much so. He became my self-appointed trainer and made me do a hundred kicks, a hundred punts and a hundred throws every day. He drove me insane with the practice, practice, practice and instead of it just being a fun goal, it became my job. I wanted to do this competition on my own, my way, but I spent the summer at Geno's Boot Camp.

Fortunately for me, while I was working on this competition, he found other outlets for his anger like exacting revenge for the time his taxi was broken into while he was parked at an OTB as he and the guys were doing their afternoon gambling.

On the day of the big competition, my best friend Barry, who I had known since we lived on Barbour Street, with his mom and dad, my aunts and uncles all turned out to see how I would do. After all, I was known both in my family and in the neighborhood as the best athlete in town among kids my age, and even among some of the older kids. I could play all positions in both baseball and football. Considering the training schedule Dad had me on, which still included all my regular maintenance chores, and how I had been training for the event, I was exhausted going in that day. My dad, right there watching, also made me incredibly nervous.

There were about ten boys in my age group, and not only did I beat all of them, but I also finished third overall. I accepted my trophy in front of cheering family and friends.

Except my father, who walked away from the stands to his car.

He didn't clap or even nod as he left.

I was heartbroken.

I had trained hard for my first competition and finished third overall out of dozens of kids and that wasn't good enough for him. If I had ever missed the million other signals, he thought I was inadequate, this one was louder than an air raid siren. All my family and friends who were there came up to admire the trophy and pat me on the back. My mom was so proud she was beaming, and she had already prepared a big "win or lose" cake at the house for everyone.

When we got home, our driveway was full of cars. Everyone who had been at the competition was already there. We all gathered in the playroom to celebrate with some of my mother's fabulous cake and ice cream. As we sat down, my father walked in and just stared at the spread Mom was putting out. He had that angry look.

I will never forget the interaction between him and Barry's mom, Janet. Janet was a loud and proud Jewish mom despite Barry being a dorky "two left feet" kind of kid with big, black plastic framed glasses whose football team nickname was "Stonehands" because he dropped more passes than anyone.

"How about your kid finishing third in his first competition?" Janet asked my dad.

Dad just gave her a blank stare as her words registered with him and he fumbled for a reply. She was not the type of woman you messed with. He just looked distant, and we all thought he was going to say something nice for once. He looked at Janet and instead said, "Third place is for losers, first place is for winners," then walked out of the room.

Janet was speechless and just looked at my mom in horror. Janet and her husband Art were always encouraging Barry, no matter what, and her expression said it all. I could tell she desperately wanted to tell my dad off but somehow restrained herself.

My mom shook the tension off with her typical grace and humor and served up the food while everyone ignored the comment and went back to celebrating.

Everyone except for me.

I heard what he said, and that moment has stuck with me to this day. I never finished third in anything I competed for again.

Not because third is for losers, but because I had something to prove to this grumpy old son of a bitch.

As they were leaving the building, they saw two guys, one Black and one white, trying to pry open the trunk of Geno's taxi with a crowbar. Back then, no one ever locked their car doors, so someone's trunk was the sacred money hole where everyone kept their valuables locked away.

These fools picked the wrong cab and time to make their move.

A couple of my dad's guys ran over to the taxi yelling and swearing as the would-be robbers attempted to flee on foot. Since they were in a crowded area, my dad's guys couldn't pull out their guns so instead, they gave chase. Had this happened anywhere less busy, these two punks would have had bullet holes all over their backs.

Dad's guys quickly caught up to the two bungling robbers and Dad said later he could tell just by the look of them they were obviously strung out on something.

This wasn't as far-fetched a theory as you might think. It was the early 1970s and acid and LSD use was commonplace.

Dad and his guys grabbed them and threw them into the trunk of one of their cars. They all set sail for The Clubhouse—one car with the two would-be burglars (who must have been sweating bullets) in the trunk. No one was ever at The Clubhouse on weekdays and as an added benefit it was just down the street from the OTB. As I have said, at this time in his life my dad had no patience or empathy for anyone or anything. Johnny K, who was there, told me he had never seen my dad so angry and evil, and he had been with my dad for years.

Tony "Porkchops" and Jim, one of the other guys, dragged these two drugged out, petty thieves into the basement and held them up against a cement wall. The gang was all still wearing their OTB suits, and no one said a word as my dad stripped down to his t-shirt and underwear.

My dad told his guys to hold the Black guy first. They grabbed him and stuffed a rag in his mouth. Dad grabbed a hacksaw on the basement floor and sawed off two fingers of this scumbag's right hand. In a matter of seconds, he was down to only eight fingers. Johnny K said my dad was possessed when he was telling my mom the story. He had a look he had never seen before. That poor drugged out guy screamed under his gag. Blood was everywhere but my dad didn't stop until he sawed off the guy's big toe as well. Then he moved on to the other guy whose mouth had been stuffed with an old rag as well. The crew scrambled around the Black guy, wrapping rags on his hand and foot to stop the bleeding.

Dad then grabbed a nearby ax and without a sound chopped off the white guy's crowbar hand. Johnny K said The Clubhouse looked like Sam's butcher shop. Finished,

Dad calmly said to the two guys, "If I ever see you again, you're dead," and walked away.

Pork Chops and Jim wrapped up the would-be robber's bloody stumps with paper bags and rags then dragged them up the stairs and out the back door of the house. They threw the punks back into the trunk of one of the cars and then literally tossed them out in the driveway of the Emergency room.

There certainly marked an evil change in my father. While he had never been a choirboy, this act signaled a crossover to a darker place. Even his guys were afraid to ruffle his feathers and were puzzled about how physically and personally ruthless he had become. In the old days my dad never got his hands dirty, he would have Sonny or one of the guys handle that kind of a thing like they did with the Dangling Man incident. This hands-on activity was certainly new behavior and after that there were many other times when my father went over the top with others who did him wrong and that included how he handled a bully I encountered one day when I was on my newspaper route.

I was fourteen then, and I had been beaten up at Southwest Park by a nineteen-year-old guy named Chuck. He and his buddies decided to knock me off my bike as I was on my paper route.

I fought them off the best I could, but I had no chance against so many boys older and bigger than me.

Chuck punched me in the mouth, splitting my lip and then he and his cohorts ran off with my papers. Stupid bully behavior kids can get away with.

I walked home with my broken bike and a bloody shirt, covered in dirt and grass.

Mom met me at the door. I wasn't crying, I was pissed.

I told her what happened, and she got out the first aid kit to stop the bleeding on my elbows and knees and patch me up. Then she called the newspaper I was delivering for and told them what happened so customers would know why they didn't get a paper that day.

Just then, my dad walked through the front door. I was bloody and mad, holding ice on my lip and when he saw me, he immediately looked angry.

"What happened?" he asked.

I told him the story. He grabbed me by the arm. "Let's go!" he said.

We jumped in the car and drove right to Chuck's house. It was dinnertime, so Chuck and his entire family was home.

Dad banged on the door. Chuck's mom opened it, but Geno totally blew her off.

"Where's your husband?" he yelled.

Chuck's mom called to the back of the house and her husband came to the door. My dad literally grabbed this guy by the neck, pulled him out from behind the screen door and threw him up against the house. The fear in this poor guy's face was real.

"Get your son," my dad yelled. "Or I bust you right here."

Chuck's father started yelling for him, as his wife's eyes nearly popped out of her head, seeing my dad pinning her husband by his neck to the house. Cocky teenage Chuck came out, puzzled.

My dad yelled to Chuck, "Stand right there," pointing to a spot in the yard.

"Okay, haul off and punch him in the mouth," my father instructed me.

I was shocked but I was still mad.

"If you run," he coldly said to Chuck, "I will pop your father in the mouth and then you."

All of Chuck's neighbors were watching. They knew me, my dad and my father's reputation. This wasn't a huge stretch. We only lived five blocks away and Geno's reputation always had a way of preceding him.

I walked up to Chuck and threw a beautiful right hook into his lip. Then a left hook; I pictured what Johnny had told me about throwing punches. Throw combinations. I threw a right-left-right series of punches. Chuck grabbed his face and ran inside, while my father let go of his dad.

"Never again," Geno said to Chuck's dad before we jumped in the station wagon and drove home to dinner.

There were no cops or any crying to the law. That was it and it was over. Older kids never bullied me after that, and I became known as someone who would protect other kids who needed protection. My friends and I later became friends with Chuck's sisters.

This is how my dad took care of bullies back then and I learned this way of handling people like that from him.

It was a simple solution that ended things quickly. Granted, it was a different time. In his own way, my dad was teaching me that you take care of yourself and never back down from someone trying to bully you. It has never happened to me again.

Geno always denied he had any issue at all except a bad temper, but it was clearly much more than that. Many who were close to him speculated the combined factors of the diabetes medication he was on, plus his untreated clinical depression contributed to his evil personality. Others thought perhaps he had an internal physical problem he wasn't letting on about. A few of his mob buddies tried to help him with his attitude but most would just tiptoe around him. Word went out to make sure any and all deals with my dad went smoothly so it was kind of a blessing he wasn't doing many deals these days, rocking the boat would cause too many problems. The guys were also concerned for my mom at home alone with him. They stopped by regularly to make sure he wasn't going crazy on us. To his credit, all of my dad's physical anger was directed to those who disrespected him and me because I was an easy target, he never directed anger at my mom.

When his gang got tired of walking around him, they simply drove the Cadillacs he had given them away. As I said earlier, his motto about people when he was on top of his game was, "If they can't do anything for me, I don't want anything to do with them."

He was learning the hard way the feeling was mutual.

"Friends" were nowhere to be found after some time. When my father's work and generosity dried up it was replaced with anger and bitterness. And since everyone knew he wasn't taking care of my mother or us, not many people felt sorry for him. Dad was like a pressure cooker, always angry, always yelling He was not a nice person to begin with but now he was unbearable, in fact, I was wounded in one of his detonations a few months after the attempted taxi robbery.

It began one Saturday morning, with my dad pounding on my door at seven o'clock, yelling at me to get up. It was time to go to work. I was a teenager and getting a bit mouthy, as my mom would say.

"Kev, get your ass out of bed. You've got work to do. Be outside in ten minutes or you'll get what's coming to you, so you better get a move on."

It was a beautiful Saturday but today's project for my dad was to customize a new false trunk box for the taxi. and I had to spend the entire day stuck in the trunk of a car, rigging up a way to move stolen property. We removed the spare tire, and he showed me what he wanted to do.

It was a pain-in-the-ass project, made worse by my father's cheapness. He never spent money on any of his projects, so I had an old bank safe deposit box as the starting point and the rest I jury-rigged out of old scrap parts and junk. The small saving grace was the trunk in that Plymouth Fury was as big as some cars on the road are today.

The box was designed to fit behind the wheel well and be hidden from plain sight. It took me hours to weld sheet metal and screw aluminum plates into the trunk to secure the box in. At only thirteen, I had become a whiz with tools and could have easily become a mechanic if I had chosen to.

Once I got going on this project, he stood back, smoked a cigar, and watched while I worked as he circled his bets in the newspaper's race section.

Mom made him give me a break for lunch. Then he took off for a few hours to the OTB while I continued to work away.

I was still in the trunk and had just laid the carpet back down when my father returned. I thought I had done a pretty good job. No one would have ever noticed the additional boxed area.

I started to complain about how it took me all day and screwed up my weekend. My dad just looked at my handiwork and ridiculed it saying, "This is a half-assed job. You don't even know how to put a screw in straight!"

I was pretty fed up with him at that point. After lying in the back of a car trunk all day, I snapped back at him. "You do it then!"

He threw his paper down and I could see he was getting ready to explode. My talking back to him drove him right up the wall.

Nobody talked back to him, especially me.

I wanted to get out of the trunk as soon as possible because I was worried, he was going to try to grab me or punch me in the arm as he often did when he couldn't get his belt off in time. As I leapt out of the trunk, I accidentally kicked the taillight and pulled the wires out of the socket, leaving the bulb hanging.

That was it; my dad went into complete berserk mode.

I wasn't sure what he was going to do, so I ran to the side of the house thinking I would be safe if I just got far enough away from him. My mom heard the commotion and stepped out of the back door.

I didn't even make it around the corner of the house when I heard something whiz by my right ear, so close I could hear it fly by. A long yellow handled screwdriver flew by my head, and I saw it stick about an inch deep into the wood on the side of the shed. I quickly zigzagged left and jumped over the bushes of my neighbor's yard. Just then, a shovel bounced off the shed right next to where the screwdriver landed but I was too scared and breathing so heavily that at first, I didn't notice the shovel had struck me in the calf.

I was bleeding down into my sneaker.

My dad had literally almost killed me with the screwdriver and when he missed with that, he threw the shovel, which luckily only hit my leg.

My mom had seen this entire event from the top of the steps of the back door and began yelling at the top of her lungs.

"Geno, what the Hell are you doing now? Trying to kill your own son, you stupid son of a bitch?!?"

She went over and picked up the shovel.

Peeking through the bushes, I only saw the fire in her eyes. She ran up to my dad, called him every name in the book and, she wound up with the shovel in her hand and I thought she was going to clock my dad on the head with it.

My dad just turned quickly and walked back to the driveway.

My mom started crying and threw the shovel across the yard. She yelled over the bushes at me.

"Kev, are you okay?"

"I got hit with the shovel," I yelled back, crawling out of my hiding spot. Blood was pouring down my leg. The shovel point had ripped a hole in my calf, and it was immediately clear I needed stitches. She ran over with a towel, wrapped my leg, and then ran into the house to grab her purse and car keys.

"Get in the car," she yelled to me. Dad just watched me limp across the yard and into her car while he tried to fix the taillight wires I had mistakenly kicked. Mom threw her purse into the car, jumped into the vehicle, and pointed at my father.

"This shit ends now! When I get back, this shit is over!" she screamed as she tore off out of the driveway.

She raced me to our local doctor who immediately took us in and stitched me up. My mother was beside herself; furious and unsure of what to do. In those days, there weren't domestic abuse hotlines or shelters. Today, with one call, the cops would have hauled him in for sure.

When we got home, I just went to my room. My mom tore into my dad, who was in the playroom, glued to the TV, watching college football. She was yelling louder than I had ever heard and never let him get a word in. Mom realized that only an inch to the left and that screwdriver would have easily punctured my skull and killed me.

"This shit ends NOW, Geno. NOW! Do you understand?" she yelled. Nothing like this is to EVER happen in MY house again. Get help or get the hell out."

There weren't many times when my mom overpowered my dad, but she won the battle that day for sure. The courage it took for her to do this, after years of seeing my dad destroy men twice his size, was incomprehensible. She was only 5'2" and one hundred and ten pounds and my father had six inches and easily a hundred pounds on her. Any misstep my dad took while she was yelling at him that day and I genuinely believe she would have killed him.

She had a good portion of Mumma in her which rarely came out but when it did, it was enough to make a grown man tremble with fear and my dad was no exception.

But she didn't strike him. When she said her piece, she just walked back into the kitchen and didn't speak a word to him for the rest of that day or many days after, for that matter.

The communication between them after this incident was never the same.

As for me, I sat in the purple walled room I had built for myself over the summer. That summer my father had decided I was old enough for my own room, but I had to spend every weekend building it off of the garage. The upside was it was private, and I could decorate it however I wanted which meant Farrah Fawcett, Susan Dey and Minnesota Vikings (or Red Sox, depending on the season) posters. I gazed at them, listening to the Osmond's and Elton John blaring from my 8-track tape player and wondered how the hell things had gotten so crazy. I never left my room. Mom brought me dinner, then cake and went to the playroom to knit while she watched TV alone. I spent hours that night contemplating why I was the target of his abuse and rage.

Those hours extended to at least a week. I didn't talk to my dad at all, not one word. I didn't have dinner with the family or join them in watching TV. I stayed in my room and listened to music and talked to my friends on the phone. I would sneak out the bedroom window and go to the kitchen for food then return. I was a tough kid, and I could take most of the crap my dad dished out. My biggest concern was getting the stitches out of my leg in time so I could compete in the next punt, pass, and kick event, which was rapidly approaching.

My mother had certainly made her point and rattled his cage enough for my dad to get his priorities straight for a while.

His battle with her over the screwdriver incident led him to acknowledge his diabetes was getting worse.

One of the first things she did was insist Dad go to a real doctor instead of Ralph, who was really nothing more than a shady (and inexpensive, which was why Geno liked him) pharmacist. The circulation in his feet had gotten really bad and he was starting to go blind in one eye. Diabetes and depression had slowed him down to the point that in his fifties, he looked like a man in his eighties. His temper was also totally out of control, and he needed to fix things quickly or Mom was leaving for sure, but she thought the right medication might help.

My father had made an appointment to go in and have a thorough physical with Dr. Gerwitz. A few days later, the doctor called with the test results. Dr. Gerwitz put him on different and stronger medications which helped him tremendously for a short while.

As for our home life, things were never the same. My dad had never apologized for anything he had ever done wrong including nearly killing me with a screwdriver and no one expected this time would be any different.

He just further distanced himself from us.

His enterprises were now suffering a full collapse. He had given his booking operation to younger guys to run although he would take his cut of it and he still fenced stolen goods from time to time, but his prime source of income was driving fares around in the taxi. These were no longer only high-end fares, just anyone that needed a ride. But his meter was still rigged, and he was certainly making more than any other cab in the city. With his health deteriorating, he knew he only had a short time left to drive and losing that money was going to be another huge hit for his income, but this didn't stop him from gambling. Any extra money just meant more cash to blow at the racetrack and Jai Alai. If he had a slow week, he would use one of his numerous credit cards for some easy cash.

My mother was furious, he wasn't giving her his cab money for the household, and she couldn't bear his stinginess on us any longer. With my brother and sister, a little older, she decided to take a job on the third shift back at the plant, so she almost never had to deal with Dad or his antics.

My mother essentially became the sole breadwinner.

This job and third shift hours contributed to my father's frustrations as well. He continued to spiral down into that dark place, and his spirit was never eviler.

Not only did my parents rarely see each other, but once again, I was called into double duty: this time running the household when my mom was working. My mother had no choice but to lean on me to help. I had to babysit, fix meals, prepare my brother and sister for bed, and still had to do my homework and help with the taxi and yard work. At only thirteen, I was given adult responsibilities, but I handled them perfectly and still managed to find time to become an excellent athlete.

By the time I was fourteen, Woodstock had happened a few years before. Times were still changing but civil rights activism had been overshadowed by anti-Vietnam war sentiment and protesters. Young people believed they shouldn't trust anyone over thirty. There was a huge societal clash between change and transition. All I knew was my father's traditions and rules weren't getting me anywhere, so I supported any kind of change which came my way.

My father treated me the same as when I became an adolescent. That made me skeptical of authority and rules in my day-to-day life and eventually grew into a full-blown disdain for "the system" and our government. I needed a pressure valve of my own, and sports, football in particular, became my outlet, especially as there were more opportunities, as I got older. A group of my friends decided that a great release was to set up an unofficial sandlot football league. We gathered the top five neighborhoods in the surrounding area and came up with a schedule. Each neighborhood would play each other every week. While it kept us busy, it was semi organized. We all just loved to play the game. It was a unique idea and everyone in high school knew who we were, it became the talk of the town. Most of us played on the high school football team and played sandlot football as well.

My dad began to feel better after the new medication. His personality came back gradually, and he was approachable for a few months after the medication kicked in. As his head cleared, he started making money and once again, he was venturing into his favorite places, the racetrack and Jai Alai.

While the new medication helped, he was still too frail to be much of a jerk, but his behavior was a little less selfish. He started doing more family activities and that summer we took a couple of weekend trips each month to places like Old Orchard Beach, Maine and Lake George, New York. Both destinations were close to racetracks, so it was another win-win for Geno. Before we set out, he would plan and work out betting deals with the few of his buddies he still had left and then he would coordinate track visits with them while he dropped us off at the beach or lake.

That was fine with us. We got to vacation at nice places, and we didn't have to deal with him much.

My dad also started giving us boys positive (for him) attention. There was a big yard behind the house, and we were allowed to build any kind of playing field we wanted there. Geno even had big spotlights installed so our backyard looked like a sports arena. Ralph and I were both becoming excellent athletes. He was a Little League star, and I was intent on playing varsity football my freshman year in high school. I made the team, even though I was young and chubby. I had a lot of talent and my punt, pass and kick accomplishments (I came in first on my second attempt) had made me a small-town hero. You would never guess it by looking at me now (I still LOVE cake but my days on the football field are long over!) that back then I was fast, could kick, had a great throwing arm, and loved to tackle.

My brother The Messiah's Little League games always took precedence over my football games, but I never complained. If you can imagine having a cigar-chomping mobster father on the sidelines, alternately talking it up to the other parents or yelling if you made a mistake, you understand why I was okay with his absenteeism. When he wasn't there, I was more relaxed. I didn't think about messing up, I only thought about playing the game.

Ralph never had to worry about that. He got nothing but sideline praise from our father.

Surprisingly, my dad was around for all my brother's sporting-events and when he wasn't at his games or practices, he was back to moving stolen goods and gambling regularly. My mom was into our athletics too and joined all these booster clubs. Our nights were spent at the ballpark or the high school for football practices. I loved the town and my friends but what was most important to me was the time I spent on the ball fields. It was the only time I felt at peace. For the first time in years, it was almost normal family life at 22 Laurel Road.

Until I had a new problem.

My football coach, Pat, was a real hard ass. He was missing a hand, which was amputated at the wrist, and we all called him "Stump," as long as he wasn't within ear shot. Pat fashioned himself after a drill sergeant but in reality, he was just a total asshole on an ego trip which mostly entailed bossing boys around. To top that off, he sucked as a coach, and I grew to hate him. It wasn't his yelling that fazed me. He was like a kitten compared to what I got at home.

I remember the first time he and my dad met.

Geno was wearing his ever-present fedora and he pulled Coach Pat aside to talk to him. No doubt my dad's reputation preceded him, and Pat knew exactly who he was. I'll never know what was said but I do know I didn't get any special treatment because of that conversation. If anything, I got it harder in practice than most of the guys. My best guess was that he told the coach not to go easy on me, to make me work.

It wasn't long into being on the team I decided I wasn't getting the playing time I wanted, even though I was only a freshman and somewhat lucky to be on the varsity team at all. I threatened to quit if I didn't get what I wanted. This did not sit well with the coach and even worse with my father.

When I told Stump that, we had a huge blow out on the practice field. I threw my helmet down and stormed off to the locker room. I'd had it with this "tough guy" bullying me. I got enough of that kind of attitude at home. Now I was the pressure which needed a valve.

My tantrum was a huge mistake. Dad was on the sidelines and saw the whole thing.

I was at my locker when the Junior Varsity coach, Mr. Scuderi, walked in. He was a rough and jacked Italian ex-football player and knew my dad all too well. I knew I was in for an ass chewing and right behind him was my father. Coach Scuderi told Dad to wait outside, he wanted to talk to me privately, and for once, my dad backed off and left us alone.

Surprisingly, for someone who always yelled, Coach Scuderi was calm and quick to point out my dad was not going to like this behavior. He also gave me a little pep talk, and with that in mind, I left for the day, planning on returning to the team tomorrow.

I left the locker room and was met by my dad's evil stare. He said nothing to me as he drove us home. I didn't get yelled at or belittled, so I thought just maybe I had gotten away with my punk, teenage behavior. That fantasy lasted until after dinner. Once we were done, Dad called me outside and handed me a shovel.

"What do you want me to do with this?" I asked.

"Start over there," my dad pointed to the back yard. "Dig a hole five feet deep by five feet wide."

"What!?!" I yelled in response.

Again, I only got The Stare. I shook my head and started digging.

Soon, I had the hole about the size he wanted. I jumped out of it and went into the house to get something to drink. When I came back, my dad was still standing there, smoking his cigar.

"Now fill it!" he yelled.

Fill it? I had a rough day already and now I came home to marine basic training. I snapped back.

"What's your problem?" I couldn't take it anymore.

Dad came over and punched my shoulder with all of his strength.

"Do it!" he hissed.

Pissed off, I filled the hole back in. After a while, I began to relax, knowing I was close to being done with this asinine punishment. By the time I was done, it was almost dark, the hole was filled, and I thought that was the end of it.

The next day I went to football practice where I got my ass chewed out for my antics the day before and had to run extra laps, but I was okay with that.

When I came home, the shovel was there waiting for me. I had to dig another hole.

It was an insane, Marine Corps punishment, not something for a kid.

I dug a new hole in a different spot, then had to fill it back in again.

I did this for seven days straight; dug five by five holes only to fill them in again.

No explanation came with it, no reasons. Just because my dad felt embarrassed by my behavior.

15. THE SUPERNOVA EXPLODES

By the time I was seventeen, my father was feeling well enough to expand into working with some of his out-of-state business contacts. The New York guys (I never knew anything more about them than that), wanted in on some of the business involving moving stolen diamonds out of Hartford. This was around the same time I wanted to have a real part-time job and start making more money than the few bucks I got from my paper route. I was a teenage boy and ready to date!

Our next-door neighbors, George and Mary, both worked for airlines which had branches at nearby Bradley International Airport. George was in management and his wife, Mary, was a very pretty stewardess. George got me a part-time job unloading the airplane baggage; a "ramp rat" is what we were called back then.

It was a tough job, but the money was great for a teenager. I didn't know my job was part of a scheme until long after I stopped working there.

My dad had known I was eager to get a real job and had been talking to George. The two of them spoke every night by the bushes. Mary wouldn't let George smoke in the house so he would routinely stand outside with my dad while they smoked their cigars. It was during one of those conversations my dad hatched another brazen win-win scheme, and he offered George a cut of the action.

Bottom line, George would let my dad know what flights were going to New York.

Only the flights to and from New York mattered to Geno.

While the plane was being unloaded and the baggage was being taken out of the belly, one of the jobs George had me do was swap out the first aid kit.

I just did what I was told, even though many of the flights came from overseas and their first aid kits were almost never touched. I would go into the belly of the plane, unlatch the first aid kit, and replace it with another. Then, I would bring the old kit to George.

It was harmless, really. At least, I thought it was; I just thought the kits had expiration dates on them or something.

My dad was always looking for a perfect scheme and boy, did he find one!

Geno was taking the diamonds his guys stole in the city, wrapping them in ace bandages, putting them inside plastic bags and giving those bags to George. George would then load them into the inconspicuous first aid kit. In those days, there was almost never a security guard around, not at all like today, so this was very easy to do. I swapped the first aid kits out in the cargo area and off to New York where they went.

There were thousands of dollars in diamonds and jewelry in each kit.

Once in New York, the ramp manager at the other airport, (George's counterpart), would have his baggage guy do the same exact thing as me. The first aid kit with the goods was then brought to the office where the New York crew would pick it up. Then they would send back money, jewels (and even drugs) in a different first aid kit.

I knew nothing about these smuggling switch offs.

Dad had paid off George and the New York crew took care of their ramp manager there.

It was foolproof. And I was living proof of that. I was the fool helping them along.

Yet another one of my dad's money-making schemes. Anything to take the easy way out and my dad would do it.

I worked that job after school for two years. I swapped out kits several times a week. Whatever they were making for money, it had to be profitable; that operation continued long after I left the job.

My father had a burst of energy during the early to mid-1970s. He tried new medications; Roger, the local pharmacy owner was a pal of his and Roger had found a new medicine called Glipizide that was being prescribed to help people with diabetes. Roger supplied my dad with this new drug in the early 1970s. Being that he and my dad grew up together he was never in danger of running out. Glipizide was a medicine that would control his diabetes. My dad would not go to a doctor, so Roger was his health advice guru. I know during those years he was doing very well financially. He even had enough money to stuff it back into his hidden cubby hole in the closet. And Glipizide was helping my dad feel much better.

But after that spurt, my dad began to slow down in the late 1970s. Glipizide had run its course, it was time for my dad to see a real doctor. His eyesight and circulation in his feet continued to become a serious issue. Even though he still treated me like a hired hand, there was a part of me who remembered him being a generous, fun, tough guy. I only had those sympathy thoughts for a short time. The sicker my dad became the meaner he was getting. That's a bold statement considering he was one of the meanest people I had ever met. As I had said, my dad rarely visited the doctor, so it was impossible to address his many issues. The few times he went was really not enough to fix all his issues. You would have thought that despite his health problems, he was making money again and that would have cheered him up, but there was no room left for solace, so his attitude and personality became meaner spirited than ever.

His protracted illness made him slow his work activities, which meant he grew more frustrated, and this led to another tension build up at home.

We all suspected there was more to Dad's illness than just diabetes or depression. He began to lose weight and became lethargic. That didn't mean that he was not grumpy, loud, or mean. He was still all of that, and in his worst moments, we would threaten to have the Gabardine Gang take me, Mom, Ralph, and Gina out, and not for a fancy steak dinner. I knew he was more than capable of acting on this threat, so while I literally feared for my life at times, I was also becoming a teenager with raging hormones and a big mouth.

Something had to give at the little ranch house at 22 Laurel Road. Years of frustrations and anger were coming to a head between my father and me. As much as I feared him in my younger days, it had been time for me to prove that I could be a man as well.

Throughout my early teens, my dad gave me no options. There wasn't a right or wrong; it was his way or the belt. Now that I was older, the belt didn't work and all he could do was yell or shoot me.

My teenage years never really got any better. I never felt safe. I knew at any time my dad could pull out his military training punishment and make me do something I hated. I had chores to do around the house every day. That's not to say that all my friends didn't have chores as well. John and Barry both had to clear the snow in their yards, but they had snow blowers, and their families weren't any better off than ours. When I asked for a snowblower I was ridiculed and told to keep my chubby ass working off the food I ate. I had to shovel by hand.

I know they never had to dig holes and fill them back in and they didn't have a daily job like cleaning the taxi out every day.

I knew the manual work I had to do was far beyond what other kids were doing and while I resented it, I could tolerate it. What was getting increasingly difficult to tolerate was the verbal and physical abuse that came along with it.

I never consciously set out to make a stand against this treatment. I knew it wasn't fair, but my discontent hadn't become action.

Like many rebellions, it started out innocently enough.

My brother and I had just bought some new curveballs on the market, essentially a rubber-coated baseball, with one side cut flat. It was shaped like that so pitchers could practice throwing curve balls. Ralph was a Little League pitcher and I liked playing catch with him so he could practice.

We were excited to try this novelty ball as soon as we got home.

I got out the 1960s Bob Montgomery catcher's mitt Detective John had given me. Bob Montgomery was a famous catcher at the time and John told me he got it from a friend of his.

The stupid mistake Ralph and I made was to set up practice in the driveway instead of the yard. We made a few tosses, but the ball was unpredictable, so much so that on one toss, I threw what I intended to be a boomerang pitch, but instead, it passed my brother's glove and went right through my dad's bedroom window.

My mom heard the breaking glass, quickly realized what had happened and she was livid. She yelled at us from the bedroom window as she scrambled about picking up the broken glass and then replaced the window with a screen, hoping my dad wouldn't notice.

We all walked on eggshells waiting for my father to come home.

The broken window was at the top of the driveway facing the entrance, so it was almost impossible for him to miss it. Sure, as the sky is blue, he noticed it right away and burst into the house yelling.

"Geno, calm down. It was just an accident. Pitches get out of control sometimes. That's why it's called 'practice'," she said as calmly as she could.

What he did next reinforced to me what I already knew that my brother was definitely his favorite child. No one had said a word about who broke the window, but my dad immediately assumed I was the culprit. Never even consider my brother. He marched right up to me. "You big buffoon," he said, using his latest word for me, never looking at my brother.

I just shook my head "no" in complete deniability then he punched me in the arm and walked away.

I was the scapegoat again.

He didn't know my brother wasn't responsible. It was simply beyond him to find fault with anyone other than me. We ate dinner and no one said a word about the window but I had a feeling my dad wasn't finished on the subject. In his mind he was thinking up some sort of punishment for me.

My brother hopped in the shower right after dinner and when he was finished, I took my turn. Being a twelve-year-old little pain in the ass, Ralph jimmied the bathroom door lock while I was in the shower, snuck in and dumped ice water over the shower curtain. I could hear him laughing as he grabbed my towel and ran out the door.

I hated that trick. Everyone who has ever been on the receiving line of that prank does.

But Ralph had gone too far that day. He had already seen my dad punch me out for something we were both responsible for. He had escaped all accountability, watched me take full blame and the punishment for it and now, he was adding insult to injury.

My rational mind knew he was younger than me and didn't understand this from my point of view.

Why would he? He had never been punished for anything; let alone to the extent I routinely was. But that day, I just wasn't in the mood to let it slide.

There was no question the only person who was going to stand up for me that day was me.

If Geno had taught me anything, especially after my paper route incident, was only I could put a foot down to bullshit thrown my way and as silly as it sounds now, Ralph's childish shower prank was the push I needed to make a stand. Looking back, I became an angry teenager.

Having been on the receiving end of many pranks like this one, I knew Ralph's next move was as predictable as the sun rising so I used that to my advantage.

I got out of the shower but left the water running as I put my pants and slippers on and hid behind the door.

Sure enough, Ralph, still hearing the shower going, thought I was in there warming up after the ice bath he had just delivered and he was primed for round two, which fell perfectly into my plan.

As I stood behind the door ready to pounce, I heard the lock being jimmied again. I knew he was never going to know what hit him and that was exactly how I wanted it. I was bigger, stronger, wiser and most of all, entirely fed up with life in general and ready for revenge. Ralph was just a gnat compared to the other annoyances (mostly my father) I had to contend with on a daily basis, but unlike other things, I could do something about this gnat.

The pressure in me, over so many things for so long, needed an outlet and this bathroom prank was a handy release.

The door opened, as I knew it would, and I sprung out from behind it, grabbed Ralph by the shirt and pushed him into the still running water. Water went flying as he hit the shower wall, ricocheted off of it and then slammed against the bathroom wall where the laundry hamper was.

Unfortunately, the living room wall was on the other side of that wall and on the living room wall was mounted a heavy bronze candle holder clock which hung right above the brand-new television my shriveled, defeated, foul tempered father with swollen feet and one good eye was watching.

I came out of the bathroom in time to see the clock come off the wall, hit the top of the TV and land on the floor.

Ralph wasted no time getting up and running away, slamming his bedroom door behind him.

My father started going ballistic, yelling at me full strength calling me a buffoon and a baby, just belittling and piling his foul temper on me until I couldn't take it anymore.

I snapped.

What happened next was like the climactic final shootout scene from every cowboy movie ever made.

My mom heard the ruckus and walked out of the kitchen as I walked into the living room where my father was walking towards me, just yelling with his big Italian mouth.

Something snapped in me at that moment.

There was nothing new in the insults and profanity my father directed toward me. I was simply past hearing them. All that was registering in my mind was incomprehensible sounds, not words. I knew what the sounds and the angry face meant, I heard and saw them for years.

They were meaningless, useless, and annoying as Hell.

I just wanted them to stop and put an end to this bullshit.

I saw my dad getting ready to punch me in the arm and before I knew what I was doing, I channeled Johnny K and uncoiled a picture-perfect right hook to his jaw.

I dropped him like a rock with that one punch.

My mom stood there helplessly, watching the entire event while I also just stood there, frozen, knowing my dad would literally kill people who even attempted this. A zillion thoughts went through my head, as he lay there groggy, trying to get up, but one thought was first and foremost.

I knew I had to go and go quickly.

He tried getting up and I saw my mom leaping over the end table in her sundress and apron, knocking over a lamp in her haste to get to him before things escalated further. She grabbed my father with one hand and tried pulling him down onto the couch as he struggled to stand.

I ran out of the house and down the street with no destination in mind other than somewhere, anywhere, else.

Back at home, my mom calmed down my dad and then snuck off. She called all of my friends to tell them about my fight with Geno and asked them to keep an eye out for me. By then, I had made my way to my high school football field and sat on a sideline bench wondering what the hell was going to happen to me.

Nobody punches someone like my dad, let alone square to the jaw, knocking him out. I knew I was in big trouble.

As I contemplated my fate, I saw a little gold Le Car and a Dodge Charger pull into the parking lot. The cars were driven by two of my friends, Alan, and John M., who had set off looking for me after my mom's call. They came down to the field, asked what happened and I told them the story.

They couldn't believe what I did and, knowing my dad, they were both afraid for me and with good reason. They took me to McDonald's and bought me dinner as I had fled the house with nothing.

No money, wallet, or even socks.

Nothing.

My only footwear was the slippers I had put on after my shower.

Alan told me to go to his house with him where we would figure something out and I could call my mother. When I reached her, I knew she had been crying and also knew I had put her in the middle of a shit storm. She told me my dad had taken off to Jai Alai. but had told her I wasn't to come back.

There was a long pause and then, with her voice cracking, she said, "Your dad has thrown you out."

"Where do I go?" I asked her, my voice cracking too.

"I'll call your Uncle Dicky in Massachusetts and see if you can stay there until we sort this out. I know a young man your age doesn't want to spend the summer in Maine with their grandmother. Plus, we both know she's not the easiest person to get along with," and even though we were both sad and frustrated, we laughed a little at her understatement.

"Now, put me on the phone with your friend's mom Patty so I can see if you can stay with them for the night. I love you. We'll work this out."

This is the one time I had stood up for myself had cost me greatly.

I was seventeen, homeless and without my parents and siblings, although Dicky quickly stepped up to the plate the next day and took me in for the summer at his house.

I was fine going there. I wanted to be with the most easy-going relative possible. I thought it would be a few months of fun before I started senior year in high school and decided whether to join the Air Force or go to college. I was very mistaken about the fun part.

As I got older family life brought with it more responsibility. I had to babysit both kids all the time, which was more or less okay, I was used to doing that for Ralph and Gina, but I had almost no time to make friends and have fun there. Dicky was the nicest guy and worked at a paper plant and his wife, my aunt Trisha, was an absolute knockout. Unfortunately, my aunt was also a woman that could not honor her marriage. She would talk to guys on the phone all the time when he wasn't around. Dicky was clueless about this, as he was to the fact that she was always making passes at me. I didn't dare say a word to him about this because I was terrified of being thrown out and having nowhere to go again. That summer was tough although my mom managed to sneak off and visit me once.

It didn't take long for my dad's guys to notice my absence and as a result, my father took a serious credibility hit with them. Since we had moved from Barbour Street, many of them had made a regular habit of stopping by in their Cadillacs to see my mom on Laurel Road as they made their way to The Clubhouse or the OTB. When they saw I was gone, and found out why, they quickly distanced themselves from my father. Most of his few remaining friends stopped working for him altogether and as a result, The Clubhouse closed down shortly thereafter.

It had taken my father this long to hit rock bottom and it wasn't that he was making much less money, his health was failing or that his family barely tolerated him.

Rock bottom for him was when he finally showed how low he could go against his own son. Growing up the gang all adored me. The core members of the Gabardine Gang had personally seen years of the worst of his bad temper and selfishness, they were totally shocked and disgusted that he had treated his own son like he did me. They never knew half the stories until my mom told them about the abuse that I had to live with. They lost all respect for him and without that respect as a leader, he had no more power in the group. As the gang evaluated my father's behavior, they agreed that he was not the man he once was. At one of their meetings, they agreed that they would split the business and take my father out of any type of leadership role. They all agreed that my father had no character, no self-control and was not to be in charge of any of the ventures, other than his airline scam which they left for him. This also meant he was home far more often than my mother cared for.

The stress of this situation started taking a toll on him. His declining health had made him weak and frail, he was virtually friendless, broke (for him) and no one at home sympathized with him.

After three months of this, my mom decided she had had enough. She told my dad I was coming home to finish high school, or she was moving out. As much as he didn't like me, he still adored her in his own way, so in his mind, he had no choice but to stay at the house and suck it up. It was awkward as you can imagine, We barely spoke a full sentence to each other for the first six months.

My summer "vacation" ended, and I came home to a place that didn't feel like home. My dad avoided all direct contact with me. As convoluted as it was, all communication between him and I went through my mother who would tell me what chores he wanted me to do.

I was more or less okay with that. The situation just became more uncomfortable.

I was afraid to do or say anything which had the slightest chance of getting me into trouble, so I spent as little time home as possible which was pretty easy, hanging out with my friends who all had cars (I couldn't afford a car at that time. What little money I made with my after-school job working as a baggage handler at the airport, was given to my mom to help with the house. I also used some of my spare time to work out, diet and prepare to enlist in the Air Force after I graduated.

My brother was back in school and remained the only person in the family who was on somewhat good terms with my dad, mostly because he knew when to suck up and when to stay clear, and as a result, he remained his favorite child. Gina, my sister, was only six or seven years old but that was old enough for her to hate our father and the feeling was mutual. She'd lock herself in her room because she never wanted to be around him, and I did my best to make it up to her by letting her use my room and stereo equipment when I was out.

For her part, my mother was making great money and would constantly remind my dad how much his business had taken a hit. She'd also secretly gotten a divorce lawyer and was waiting for my dad to screw up one more time, which was a certainty.

My dad's luck at staying on the straight and narrow ran out only a few months later during a Sunday night dinner. He was in his usual foul mood and was having a problem finding someone to take it out on.

I was no longer much of a target. He and I barely spoke. He couldn't berate me because I didn't give a shit at that point. The belt was no longer an option; I was way too big for that now.

Ralph and my mom were out of the question, for obvious reasons.

So, my dad, needing to turn on someone, went after my chubby, cross-eyed little sister.

"Gina, slow down. You're making a mess with your food, you fat pig. I thought this buffoon over here," pointing his knife at me, "was bad but you take the cake, you worthless kid."

I couldn't believe he was throwing the same insults he had given me for years onto my sister, a little six-year-old girl. My mom reached her boiling point.

"Shut your mouth, Geno," she snapped. "How dare you talk to a baby and your own daughter like that!"

He was quiet for about ten seconds before he started on her.

"You would be nothing if I didn't marry you!" he screamed at my mother. My dad at this time was at an all-time low, and he would not shut up threatening my mother.

My mom had given him one more shot, and he was using his mulligan now. It was getting ugly once again. The stress level was extremely high. Gina left the dinner table crying and ran to her room.

Ralph and I got up to go to the living room to escape and watch the football game and as I entered, I heard a crash behind me.

Mom had thrown a big platter of roast beef at my dad's head. He dodged it and it crashed against the kitchen wall. My dad got up from his chair, yelling at her, and then he walked to the living room to his chair. Mom was as mad as I have ever seen her. She yelled loudly from the kitchen. I couldn't understand exactly what she was saying but her message was clear:

"Pack your bags. You are gone."

My dad's temper kicked in as I was attempting to ignore the chaos around me and focus on watching the game. I looked at my brother and even he was showing signs of fear. Then, my dad crossed the line with the worst threat I had ever heard.

"You'll be dead tomorrow if you keep it up," he shouted back to her.

This enraged my mom, and a rolling pin came flying out of the kitchen, hitting the side of his chair.

Ralph cleared the room at this point. I got up and walked into the kitchen doorway to support my mom.

"I promise you, by tomorrow," he yelled.

I could hear Mom crying and this time, I'd had enough.

No more chances. This had to end.

I was going to kill my father. I had in my mind that all the years of this shit had come to boiling point.

I walked to the couch and grabbed him by his shirt. I lifted him out of the chair and without a beat, I was holding this one-time mobster in the air with both hands.

I looked him dead in the eyes.

I had nothing to lose.

If I killed him, at least Mom could live a happy life. My brain was screaming, "Kill him, choke him out. This piece of shit has treated you like shit all your life, end his."

I was eye to eye with the devil, but this time, I was not backing down. As I looked into his eyes, I could see that my father had no soul. He was completely blank inside. It was like looking into the soul of a serial killer. Experts say you cannot see anything behind the eyes of someone truly evil. I was bigger than him now, I was much stronger, and I had a temper which easily matched his. He would have to kill me to stop me.

My Italian and Irish blood were now a river of fury running through my veins and everything around me was a blur. I could see in his eyes he knew I was not "little Kevy" anymore and his rage turned into fear.

It felt like I held him there for an hour, though it was only a few seconds. I looked at Mom and while she was still crying, she gave me a small "no" nod. I knew what she meant.

My brain slowly reasoned with itself. Snapping his evil neck was not worth going to prison for.

I reached into the depths of my soul and yelled out loud, "You will never threaten to kill my mother!" in my deepest pre man voice. I had never heard this voice coming from me before. I quickly spun and threw him back into his chair like a rag doll.

"Pack your bags, you have fifteen minutes," I snapped as I started to come down from this adrenaline rush.

As I walked him into his room, I grabbed the baseball bat I kept behind my door and kept it with me. I walked him back to his room and I watched him toss some clothes together and leave the house without saying a word.

Mom and I were both exhausted and we just went to our rooms, not saying a word.

My father had blown his last chance. And he was seriously lucky to be alive.

I had been so close to killing him with my bare hands, I have never forgot that emotion and I was never the same again. Something inside me that day said to be prepared to kill or be killed. It was something that I can't explain. Many experts say that everyone has the ability to kill. I know exactly where that place in your mind is.

16. STARBURST TO BLACK HOLE

Once the dictator of the House of DiBacco fell, our family dynamic changed. On the upside, we were free from his endless demands, leeches I had once called relatives and foul disposition. I had finished high school and started taking classes at Asnuntuck Community College where I took a few classes and had a thirty hour a week work study job as a videographer/editor. But this honeymoon was quickly replaced with reality.

Rena was now the head of the household, a role she wasn't familiar with, despite years of helping my dad out with everything. She had no idea about the ins and outs of managing a home as well as organizing and paying the bills, but she was all in. God bless her, she knew our survival depended on her. She continued to work the third shift and baked wedding cakes to help make ends meet. She never quit trying and working as hard as she could to keep us afloat and together.

For his part, my dad continued on his path of being a selfish, callous, and vengeful son of a bitch and he was dead set on making my mother fall flat on her face.

He quickly adapted to single life and moved into a small apartment in a nice building with a doorman and valet parking and continued to go to the track and Jai Alai, dropping rolls of money.

Mom and us kids at 22 Laurel Road no longer existed for him.

Meanwhile, his attorney, Mr. Stein (another one of his mob connections) had acted quickly as soon as Geno moved out. He had my dad transfer all of his cash, credit cards and all other assets into Arturo's daughter's accounts, long before my mother filed for divorce and financial support.

There were two results from this action.

When he appeared in court, it looked like he had next to nothing, he cried poor. In reality he gave my cousins all his money. when the judge issued a temporary support order. As a result of these shenanigans, my mother only got eighty dollars a week to support three children and manage all the household expenses.

Secondly, this action made my cousins, Leslie and Janet, "love" him even more and spurred their willingness to help him. At his and his lawyer's request, the two of them submitted false statements of abuse, neglect, infidelity, and any other trumped-up charges against my mother they could think of to the court. He also canceled his life insurance policy and the homeowner's insurance, which in turn, made the bank begin to take foreclosure actions on 22 Laurel Road.

I left college after only one semester to help my mother as best I could, although I was limited after I slipped a disk weightlifting and that slowed me down for quite a while. I always felt terrible that I couldn't contribute more during that time.

All that work and stress took a toll on my mother and aged her considerably, but she kept doing what she had to do to keep our family together. When I look back on who was the tougher of the two, no doubt my mother was by far.

It didn't take long for my father to convince Arturo and his family that my mom was solely responsible for the failure of their marriage, and they believed this mountain of bullshit. We became totally isolated from Geno's side of the family, despite them having been constants in our lives for as long as I could remember. He even got my aunt Barbara to take his side. Geno had always given Barbara money whenever she needed, so in her mind, staying on his gravy train was far more important than any loyalty to her sister.

Once word got out what he had done to us, any friends he had left, including Johnny K disowned him. He quickly went from being the crew leader and feared mobster to the scum of the city. The only people who had anything to do with him continued to be my cousins, Leslie, and Janet. In their ignorance and selfishness, they decided to shun my mother and us because they knew that by doing that, they would be the ones to profit from my father's infamous bouts of spontaneous generosity.

Windsor Locks became a battlefield between DiBacco vs. DiBacco, not unlike Hatfield's and McCoy's. My cousins and their friends would drive by our house regularly, trying to spy on us, but my friends and I would have nothing of this and would throw baseballs at their cars every chance we got. Our "gangs" would frequently confront each other, and fights were breaking out all over town while the fights in the courtroom continued.

Overall, these courtroom trips were costing my mother thousands of dollars simply to get what was hers and it was exhausting her and wearing her down.

Finally, my dad played his trump card. We had all known he hadn't been in his right mind for years and even the most generous of explanations ("He's just selfish," "You know he's always been a gambler") were unsatisfactory. He revealed in court he had stage three Lymphoma, and it was breaking down his system. My family and I viewed this revelation as just another "poor me" ploy from him to get people on his side. While his lawyer played the dying man card, us, and other people who knew him would hear nothing of it. Even with this news, our neighbors, friends and even all the members of his old gang considered him a small, small man and hated him for acting like a spoiled, petulant child and not living up to his responsibilities.

In the end, the divorce mess yielded almost no help for my mom other than finally freeing her from him. My father had virtually no assets on paper, having disposed of them months before. Her lawyer managed to get the bank to put the house solely in her name, but only under the condition she paid off the three refinancing mortgages my dad had taken out on the house without her knowledge or consent. She never saw a dime from these loans but was still held responsible for repaying them. Mentally beaten up at that point, the bombshell of these additional debts was just too much for her. She couldn't afford the monthly payments for everything, even if we all pitched in so she decided to sell the house and just move away.

My father and his deviant, greedy relatives had accomplished what they set out to do, break my mom down and leave her penniless. I learned a long time ago that you never get what you want out of life, you get what you work for. I was able to use my childhood to motivate me to be successful in other ways.

After the divorce was final, my father got extremely ill and was told he had less than a year to live. With the house on the market, I helped my mother plan every chess move she made as she started looking at more affordable places and quickly moved to Enfield, Connecticut.

Shortly after the divorce, Geno had surgery to remove the cancerous lymph nodes and amputate his leg due to diabetic gangrene. He couldn't take care of himself, and he had no one to help him. I visited a few hospices on his behalf, finally doing all the paperwork and putting money down to get him admitted to a facility in Enfield, but he never made it there.

Dying, my father spent his last days virtually alone.

His nieces had used the assets he had put into their names to buy nice houses in nice neighborhoods for their families. Once he was of no more use to them, they forgot all about my father, their rich and charming uncle as he slowly wasted away.

While we never reconciled with him, out of respect, Ralph and I visited him after his surgeries. My mother and Gina wanted no part of him, and we couldn't blame them.

I admit respect wasn't the only reason I wanted to see him. There was no way, dying or otherwise, I was going to let him off the hook for the years of mistreatment of me, my sister and finally, my mother, had been on the receiving end because of him. I made it a point to say directly to his face, "You are going straight to Hell for what you've put Mom through," I said to this puny, dying minor league mobster, my father. "And that is going to be exactly what you deserve."

I have no guilt for telling him off like that and even today, I feel nothing; just numb when I think back on all these stories.

My father passed away only a couple of days after we visited him for the last time.

He was a man who, at one time, commanded the attention of everyone in the city. He was the mean and ornery king of organized crime in Hartford, and no one dared to cross him.

Now he had left the world with an amputated leg, lymphoma in his neck, chest, and lungs, blind in one eye and weighing about one hundred and fifty pounds. This guy who had been the boss was no longer the boss. He had no crew, no friends, no family and no one to boss around.

It was a cold snowy December day when my father was lowered into the ground at the Windsor Locks cemetery. Ironically, the only people who showed up were my brother, myself, Detective John Burns and his wife, my father's brother, Arturo, and his wife.

That was it.

Just the six of us.

Not his nieces or nephews, not one member of his crew. There weren't any friends of the great gangster. No one cared enough to show up and pay their respects.

After being a cold-hearted prick his whole life, my dad died with very few people who cared which was fitting for someone who had only ever cared about himself.

As I said at the beginning, you can only play the cards you are dealt. However, how you play them is entirely up to you. My father played the cards he was dealt with in the worst conceivable way and ended up being someone who was completely self-centered, no matter who got hurt or who was in the way.

In the end, Geno DiBacco, leader of the Gabardine Gang got treated the way he treated others.

AFTERWORD

The truth about my dad, both professionally and personally, never really sank in with me until many years later.

I didn't live in a bubble after we moved to Windsor Locks.

It was pretty easy to know my dad didn't have a job like any of my friend's dads did. Of course, I knew about his gambling but for a long time I just thought it was a hobby and not his livelihood. I knew he always had the guys around, but especially those in his inner circle, were people he had known since childhood, and I knew them throughout my childhood as well. They were just old friends like anyone's old friends as far as I knew. As far as the violence I heard about or even occasionally witnessed, it was just the guys sticking up for each other because that was the right thing to do. I didn't know they were on Dad's payroll and that loyalty was part of the job description.

In my mind, my father went from someone who was able to show passion and affection to a man stuck in the deepest and darkest places a person can ever reach.

Now my memories are clouded with the knowledge he was not a nice man, a kind man or a man who ever showed any sympathy toward anyone.

It took no time for my mother to forget him, and she had the best reason of all. For almost twenty years she had put up with him and stood by him, even when men who had reputation of being made from much sterner stuff had reached their breaking point with him.

Rena had done all she could to keep our family together. She had left him for three months in Maine, the time of the infamous Mumma shotgun incident and she had come close to it a dozen times after that. Plain and simple, back then, that's what you did when you had kids. You stuck it out as best you could, even when your finances were in shambles and verbal, as well as physical abuse fouled the atmosphere of the household.

It was hard and painful for Rena to shoulder all of this, but that was what was done. To do anything else would have shown a lack of character and my mother was far too much of a lady to allow that to happen.

After she moved to Enfield, she got a job at the Federal Reserve Bank, and she worked there for thirty years. There were a few solid boyfriends in her life during that time, but she never remarried. I think she had had enough of men after my dad, and she was simply happy to do her own thing.

She retired to Maine near where Uncle Dicky had moved. He helped her find a little cottage to rent and she had a couple of years of peace as a painter before she became ill with kidney cancer.

That didn't slow her down. Like every obstacle she had ever faced, she just adapted and took what life gave her. Despite this, she kept painting for therapy and to keep her creative brain active. Gina, Ralph, and I moved to Maine to be near her in her last years. We all felt it was the least we could do for her because we were so helpless when the worst of her years with my father were happening. That's the time when she started telling me these stories and filling in the blanks about my crazy childhood.

My sister and I were at her bedside the night she passed and while there won't ever be a greater pain in my heart than losing her, I am comforted knowing she's no longer suffering, even though she was the toughest, most resilient person I've ever known.

Without a doubt, it was hard for me after Ralph was born and we moved because I could remember when I wanted for nothing and was the little prince of Barbour Street whose father had the respect (or fear) of everyone I knew. That life was day and night from how my life in Windsor Locks evolved. But I just have to keep pushing forward.

Like I've said, you are born into a family and have to play the hand you are dealt.

Because of that, when I look back on my childhood in Windsor Locks, I played the hand I was dealt. My father was not a nice man and even a worse father. Being the first born, I took the majority of the abuse. We can't choose our parents. I would never wish the life I had on anyone. My mother was a saint, my dad was Satan. Who knows what would have happened if I had a normal father. I may not have had the motivation to succeed as I do. However, he was as bad as they come. He caused me endless nights of anxiety. I can sit here today and become obsessed about the hate I have for my father. Let the anger simmer, what good does it do me now. I tell my story, let others decide. It's not like I can go back in time and magically fix my life. Much of my career I've Interviewed people that had it much easier than I did in life only to become lifelong felons complain about their parents and end up as unproductive people in our society. I was able to use all that pain to motivate me to become successful. That is how I handled it.

I know my mother would be proud of me writing this book and telling these stories we used to talk about. She knew better than anyone how unusual a life I had. Growing up as the son of a small-time gangster is not something that happens to many people.

For more news about Kevin DiBacco, subscribe to our newsletter at *wbp.bz/newsletter*.

Word-of-mouth is critical to an author's long-term success. If you appreciated this book, please leave a review on the Amazon sales page at *wbp.bz/tgg*.

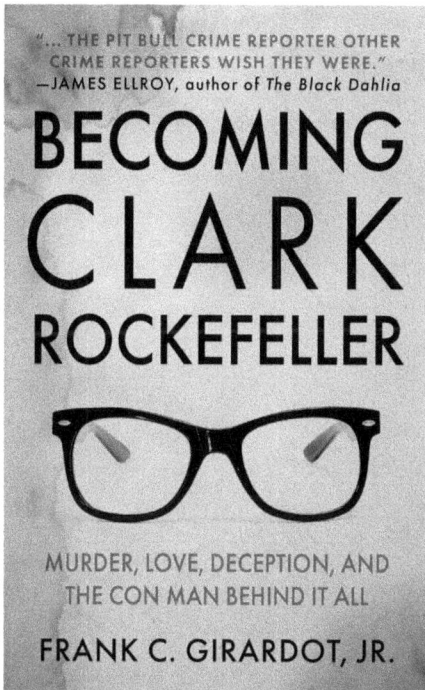

"... THE PIT BULL CRIME REPORTER OTHER CRIME REPORTERS WISH THEY WERE."
—JAMES ELLROY, author of *The Black Dahlia*

BECOMING CLARK ROCKEFELLER

MURDER, LOVE, DECEPTION, AND THE CON MAN BEHIND IT ALL

FRANK C. GIRARDOT, JR.

https://wbp.bz/bcr

BECOMING CLARK ROCKEFELLER: Murder, Love, Deception, and the Conman Behind It All delves into the life of a young immigrant entangled in a multi-generational murder investigation ensnaring some of the wealthiest Americans. Posing as bogus aristocrat Clark Rockefeller, he duped the affluent, leaving a trail of deception and national headlines in his wake.

ALSO AVAILABLE FROM WILDBLUE PRESS

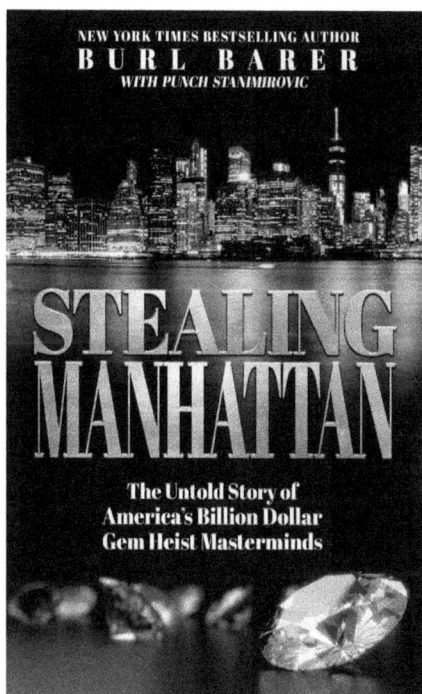

https://wbp.bz/manhattan

The true crime story of a family of altruistic jewel thieves and four decades of daring capers and sweet escapes, including a 1992 New York mega-heist.

Punch Stanimirovic insists: "My father, known as Mr. Stan, is the greatest gentleman thief who ever lived—a true genius."